The Paper Home

The Paper Home

TABLES, CLOCKS, BOWLS AND OTHER HOME PROJECTS MADE FROM PAPER

LABEENA ISHAQUE

PHOTOGRAPHY BY JANINE HOSEGOOD

jacqui small

First published in 2008 by Jacqui Small LLP
7 Greenland Street
London NW1 0ND

Text copyright © Labeena Ishaque 2008
Photography, design and layout copyright © Jacqui Small 2008

Publisher Jacqui Small
Editor Judith Hannam
Art Director Sarah Rock
Photography Janine Hosegood
Stylist Labeena Ishaque
Production Peter Colley

ISBN : 978 1 906417 01 7

2010 2009 2008 2007
10 9 8 7 6 5 4 3 2 1
Printed in Singapore

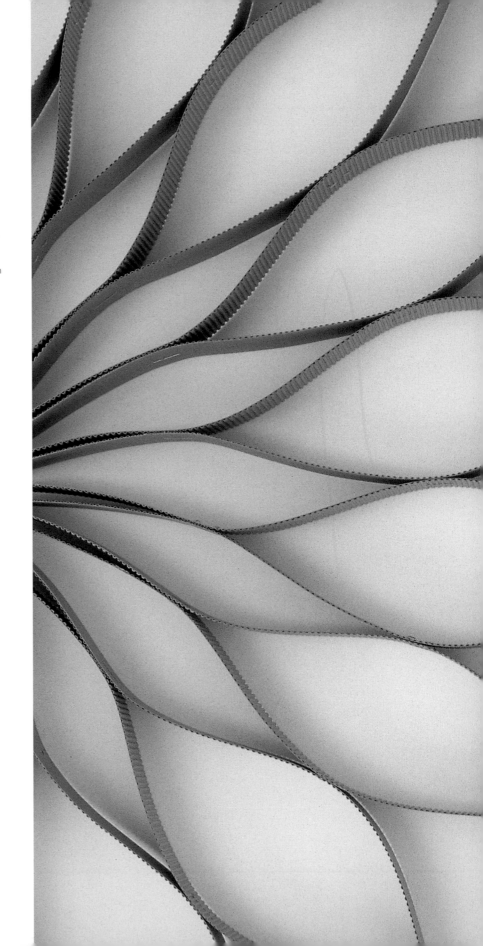

PAGE 2 An inspiring array of
textured, dyed and patterned
papers from around the world.

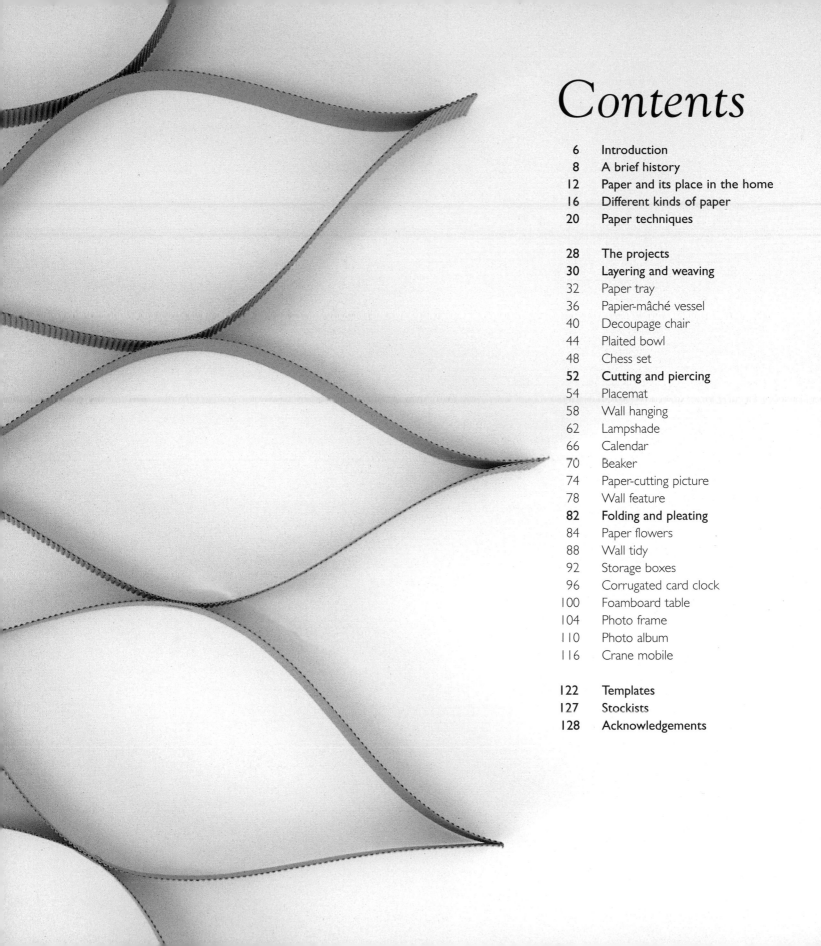

Contents

Introduction

Paper. It's a simple and humble material, yet it has a fascinating history that spans the world, as well as many generations and cultures. Variations of paper have been used for centuries, both as an art and writing material. Over time, it has evolved into something that has many uses, from the very basic to the completely decadent, and it is almost impossible to imagine life without it – no books, newspapers, pound notes and dollar bills or even loo roll.

In recent years, the massive development of electronic media systems has seen a corresponding decline in the need for paper as a communication device. As a result, alternative uses are increasingly being found for this versatile and creative material. Although initially an instrument of communication, it has developed and will continue developing as a material with many uses beyond those for which it was first invented.

Even though many see only its somewhat temporary or disposable nature, paper has long been used in the home – and not just to decorate walls. However, as its practical, durable and constructive qualities are being rediscovered, there has been a steady flow of paper interior products onto the market.

It is this versatility that has seen paper used to make everything from the traditional Japanese lanterns and folding shoji walls, to the carefully hand-painted and gilded wallpapers of the aristocratic European courts in the fourteenth and fifteenth centuries. Paper furniture, both made from papier mâché and decorated in the craft of decoupage, was popular in the homes of fashionable Victorians. Many of these pieces of furniture have survived to the present day, which is an illustration of just how durable paper is as a construction material.

Today, paper is enjoying a resurgence of popularity in interiors. This is partly due to the fact that there is an increased focus on substance and ethics in the interiors industry. As a result, using recycled and recyclable materials, such as inexpensive and utilitarian paper and card, is viewed as important and morally sound. There is also a more frivolous side to interior design, which is seeing a return of the highly decorative. Again, paper is the perfect material. New laser-cutting techniques, which allow cuts to be done with the press of a button, have enabled designers to create intricate paper lampshades and screens. The current vogue for historical and retro wallpapers, and the bright colours and funky patterns of modern designs – the likes of which have only previously been seen in textiles – has also contributed to paper's popularity.

In this book, I have demonstrated some of the almost endless possibilities of paper as a material to make beautiful projects for the home – both decorative and practical. I have used a wide variety of papers, ranging from lightweight tissue papers and old newspapers to heavyweight Indian khadi papers and corrugated cardboards, to illustrate how different kinds of paper can be employed using a range of techniques to create inspired objects for your home.

OPPOSITE A selection of handmade and machine-made papers showing variations in colour, texture and tone. The papers with rougher edges and layers, and of differing thicknesses, are handmade, while those with smoother, straighter edges are machine-made.

A brief history

When we first think of the origins of paper, it's quite natural to make the connection with ancient Egypt; the word 'paper' derives from the name of the reedy grass plant, papyrus, that the ancient Egyptians used to produce writing material. Thin layers of the plant's stem were layered at right angles to each other to make a mat; these were then soaked in water to extract the natural gum that acted as a bonding agent for the papyrus 'paper', which was then pressed, dried in the sun and rubbed with a stone to achieve a smooth surface. These sheets were not only suitable for writing and drawing upon, they were also lightweight and portable, making them ideal for record-keeping and spiritual texts. In addition to the Egyptians, both the ancient Greeks and the Romans used papyrus in this way.

On the other side of the world, in the central Americas and Polynesian islands, similar processes were taking place at a similar time. Bark mats, known as tapa, made by beating fine bark over logs to flatten it, were used for book making, painting on and also for making clothing.

These early versions of writing materials can be seen as predecessors of paper (since they were used for the same purposes), but they were more like laminated mats, rather than fine, porous sheets. Although archaeological evidence suggests there may have been something similar made at a slightly earlier date, the man credited, in 105 AD, with the invention of paper as we know it today was a court official of the Chinese Han Dynasty called T'sai Lun. Looking for a less expensive alternative to the silk scrolls that had previously been used to write on, T'sai Lun experimented with a ground-up blend of mulberry bark, hemp, linen rags and water, which he boiled up in a large vat until the fibres separated and then mashed into a pulp. This pulpy mixture was then scooped out of the vat using a framed screen made from bamboo and cloth, which allowed the water to drain out whilst catching the broken-down fibres. The dryish pulp was then pressed and flattened onto the screen, and left to dry and become bleached by the sun. The result was a sheet of thin, flexible and strong paper, known at the time as T'sai Ko-Shi: Distinguished T'sai's Paper. It has been recorded that one of it's earliest uses, apart from as a writing material, was as Imperial toilet paper.

For centuries, the Chinese kept the art of papermaking a secret from the West. Gradually, however, the knowledge dispersed. Initially, it spread slowly, south and east, through a peacetime Chinese nation, creeping, by the third century, into Cambodia, Tibet and Korea, and, by the sixth century, into Japan. It also later reached India via Nepal. Its westward migration began in about 750 AD, at a time when the Chinese Tang Dynasty was warring with the Islamic world. Following a battle along the Tarus River, a community of Chinese papermakers were taken prisoner, whisked away to Samarkand and put to work not only producing but also teaching the art of papermaking.

As papermakers made their way further west through the Muslim world – to Baghdad, Damascus and Cairo – the

OPPOSITE Rolls of paper from around the world showing the different textures available, from the smoothest, softest Japanese washi (second row, third from left), to the pulpy, veiny finish of a handmade khadi (second row, second from left).

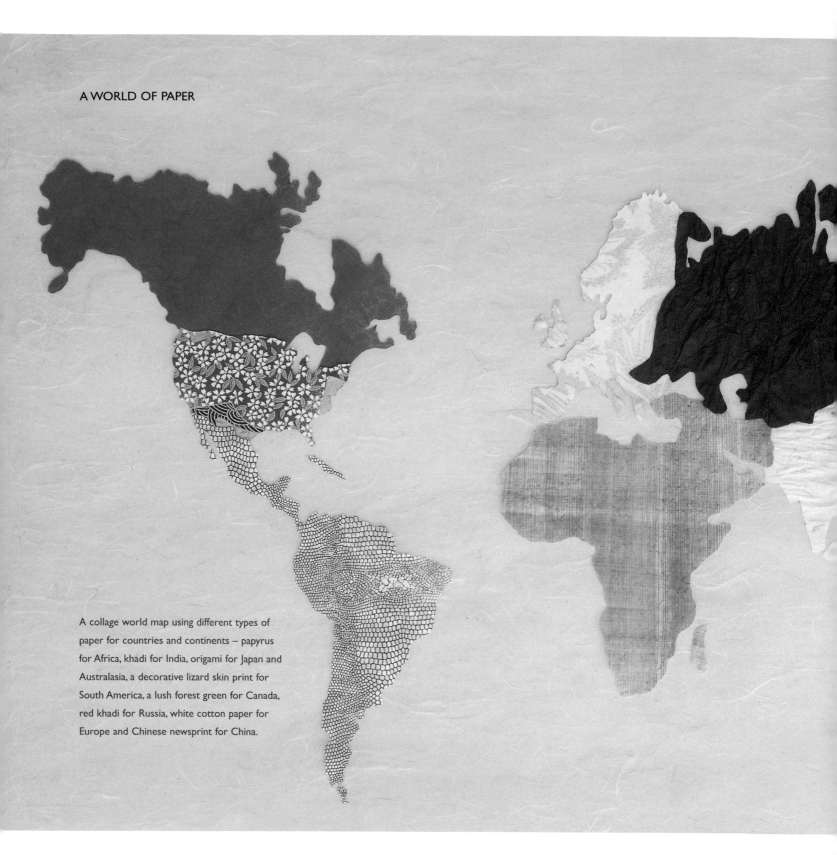

A WORLD OF PAPER

A collage world map using different types of paper for countries and continents – papyrus for Africa, khadi for India, origami for Japan and Australasia, a decorative lizard skin print for South America, a lush forest green for Canada, red khadi for Russia, white cotton paper for Europe and Chinese newsprint for China.

once secret Oriental skill became known throughout the world, finally reaching Europe in the twelfth century when the North African Moors invaded Spain and Portugal. The first known paper mill in Europe was in Spain, but the technology spread rapidly and soon there were mills throughout the Mediterranean countries, finally arriving in northern Europe in the fourteenth century.

In Europe, the use of papyrus as a writing material had reduced notably in the ninth century. The preferred medium for the artists, scholars and writers of the time was smooth vellum or parchment. However, both these materials, which were made from animal skin (calf, kid, lamb or sheep), were extremely expensive. A single Bible, handwritten on parchment, required the skins of some 300 sheep. Interestingly, the Church banned paper at first, deeming the papermaking process to be a 'pagan' art and only animal parchments holy enough to carry the sacred Word. However, economics soon reversed this decision.

Paper did not, however, become an everyday item until the fifteenth century – more specifically 1456, the year in which the German Johann Gutenberg invented movable type and printed his eponymous Bible, simultaneously spreading the word of Christianity and sparking a revolution in mass communication. This date is commonly acknowledged, in the West at least, as the beginning of the modern paper and printing industry.

By now, Europe had a thriving papermaking industry and paper was being used for printing not only Bibles but also legal documents and other important books and records. By the late fifteenth century England had begun making large supplies of paper and for many years supplied the colonies, including America. Made mainly from canvas and linen rags – and called rag bond – the paper was durable, sufficiently absorbent for inks and fairly long lasting. In fact, there was such a huge demand for rags in England at that time that the rag trade thrived as a sideline to the paper industry. Some historians go so far as to suggest that the Plague, which originally swept Europe in the fourteenth century, re-entered England on its second sweep in the seventeenth century via old, contaminated rags imported from Europe for the paper trade.

The use of rag bond continued until the eighteenth century, when cotton rags, which were more plentiful than linen, were added to the mix. Rag pulp, however, became an increasingly expensive source of fibre and, as the demand for cheap paper grew to keep pace with the development of print technology, a new source of fibre was found in the form of wood pulp. By the mid-nineteenth century wood had replaced rags to become the main ingredient of paper and remains so today.

Paper and its place in the home

The impact of paper on daily life is immense – millions of tonnes of the stuff are made and used in myriad ways every year. At the very core of paper's appeal is its versatility – the fact that it can be cheap or expensive, permanent or disposable, as light as a feather or as tough as old boots. The way it is treated in manufacturing dictates how it will react in certain situations. Although it is easy to burn, it can be made fire retardent; although it can decompose in water, it can also be made water resistant, and has been used to build the hulls of boats; it can also be strong enough to withstand acid, yet soft enough to wipe a baby's bottom.

Increasingly, as it is used less as a writing device, paper has taken on more resonance as a building and creative material. In Japan, it has always held its own within the interior environment and has been used to make a variety of items from partitions and sliding walls to lanterns and lamps. The paper most commonly used for these items is washi, a generic Japanese term describing any paper made by hand in the traditional way from the mitsumata shrub, which is also known as the paper mulberry. Unique to Japan ('wa' means Japanese and 'shi' means paper), washi is a fine, durable, insect-resistant paper that is available in most weights and textures and is ideal for lighting and screening as its translucent qualities create a soft diffused light.

Washi is also the paper most often used for the traditional Japanese art of origami, which translates directly as 'paper folding'. The wood pulp used in its manufacture is much tougher than that found in ordinary paper and as a result it can withstand many folds and creases without tearing or disintegrating.

Paper has also been used in a decorative way in the home, especially as a wall embellishment, since its invention and the use of a type of wallpaper can be traced back to China in 200 AD, when rice paper was pasted onto walls. Wallpaper in the strictest sense, however – decorated paper made using the printmaking technique – first became popular in Europe in the fifteenth century during the Renaissance period. At this time, only the most wealthy members of society could afford to hang rich tapestries, so the less well off members of the gentry mimicked them in a less expensive manner by hanging painted panels of paper, made to look like tapestries. These papers featured images similar to those found on tapestries: panoramic views of landscapes, hunts, gardens and Biblical stories. Artists also painted pieces designed to be pasted straight onto a wall, some of which consisted of several pieces of paper that had to be jigsawed together to match up the pattern, very much like a modern-day paper with a repeat pattern.

Wallpaper became particularly popular in England in the early sixteenth century after Henry VIII's break with the Catholic Church over his divorce from Catherine of Aragon led to a fall in trade between England and Flanders, where many of the tapestries came from. The lack of tapestries encouraged people to look elsewhere for their wall decorations and hence gave rise to an increase in the production of wallpaper.

OPPOSITE These paper beakers (see page 70) are made from layers of tissue paper moulded over an existing beaker. Place a glass tumbler inside, fill with water and simply add flowers.

During the seventeenth century, the Chinese responded to the European demand for wallpaper and the trade in Chinoiserie-inspired and hand-painted papers became a thriving industry. By the mid-eighteenth century, however, Britain was once again the leading wallpaper manufacturer in Europe, exporting vast quantities throughout the world.

Although wallpaper has been in and out of fashion since then, it is currently much in vogue. New printing and colouring methods that allow for photographic and light reflective finishes are driving the wallpaper business to a more futuristic and once again popular and fashionable level. The UK remains a well-respected producer of wallpaper, with a range of companies that include traditional manufacturers such as Cole and Son, as well as those that produce more fashionable, hip designs, such as Timorous Beasties and Tracy Kendall. America has its share of wallpaper companies, too, including Rollout Custom Wallpaper, which produces modern graphic wallpapers, and Flavor Paper, which makes retro-style and funky wallpapers.

It is not possible to talk about paper in a home environment without a brief mention of the illustrious history of papier mâché. A product derived from waste paper, it was invented in the Far East as long ago as 200 AD. For centuries, it has been used to make small decorative items, such as boxes and bowls. (Strengthened with many coats of lacquer, it was also used as a protective layer on Chinese helmets.) An inexpensive alternative to wood, with the possibility of being manipulated into a variety of shapes and forms, the art form was embraced enthusiastically in Kashmir and India, where beautifully lacquered and hand-painted papier-mâché trinkets can still be found, eventually moving through to Europe via the silk and spice trading routes.

By the time it reached Europe in the seventeenth century, papier mache had developed considerably and was not only being used to produce trays, screens, tableware and buttons, but also furniture and imitation stucco and architectural plaster mouldings and panels for interiors. It was further developed into a style called 'Japanning', by lacquering it intensely until it was as strong as wood and looked very Japanese in style.

At the famous 1852 Great Exhibition in London's Crystal Palace, papier mâché was heralded as the material of the future, and exhibits of a cot, chair and even a piano were put on show. By the early twentieth century, however, papier mâché was viewed merely as a pastime, and the industry appeared to be in terminal decline, unable to compete with the brash newcomer on the block: plastic. Now, with the renewed interest in all things recyclable, coupled with the inexpensive nature of the raw materials, papier mâché is again coming into own. Like other ancient paper traditions, it's been invigorated by new technologies. Indeed, a quick browse on the internet reveals that it is possible to purchase chairs, tables, cupboards and shelving constructed solely from card and paper derivatives.

It truly is a time that paper is coming home.

LEFT A wall covered in a patchwork of samples from traditional British wallpaper manufacturer, Cole and Son. This collage showcases some of their back catalogue, as well as new designer collaborations and experiments with flock and metallic finishes.

Different kinds of paper

Paper today is usually either handmade or machine-made. The traditional, handmade approach has changed little from the way paper was made by the Chinese in the first century: pulp is poured into a deckle and mould to create individual sheets. This type of paper is much stronger than machine-made, as the fibres of the latter tend to lie in only one direction, so the strength of the material is greatly diminished. A good handmade paper, however, can last for centuries.

A variation on handmade paper is mould-made paper. Similar to handmade paper, it only has two deckle edges, not four; watercolour papers are usually mould-made.

Machine-made paper is used on an industrial scale for printing books and newspapers, as well as for mass packaging. Tissue paper, cartridge paper and corrugated cardboard are all machine-made.

The following is a brief description of the different types of paper used for the projects featured in this book, so you can make an informed decision on which paper you would like to use. The paper ingredients for the projects are a suggestion and some projects can be adapted to incorporate different kinds of paper.

1 Khadi paper is made from recycled cotton rag and has been handmade by craftsmen in India for centuries. Considered particularly environmentally sound, since no machines are involved and air pollution is close to zero, the dyes for the paper are all natural. Nor is bleach used – the whitening of the paper is achieved naturally by laying it out in the sunlight. It can be produced in a range of thicknesses, but it often has some textured imperfections on the surface. It is also harder to fold than a machine-made paper, as the direction of the fibres is totally random, thus there is no warp or weft allowing for a sharp crease. (In machine-made paper, the direction of the fibres is much more regulated, lying in pretty much the same direction, so the paper has more 'give'.)

2 Card stock is a stiff or rigid paper. It's often used for postcards, brochure covers and in particular for scrap-booking and making greetings cards. The texture is usually smooth, but it can also be textured, metallic or glossy. Available in a range of weights and densities, the standard thickness used in crafting is 1–1.5 mm.

3 Rakusui paper is a Japanese mould-made paper, with a smooth, white, translucent, veil-like appearance. It is made by taking the still-wet paper and placing it over a slightly raised patterned surface, which is then rained with droplets of water, hence its name, which means 'rain paper' in Japanese. A small number of the fibres are washed away, allowing a pattern to develop in the paper. These papers are sometimes referred to as lace papers because their regular transparent patterns resemble lace cloth.

4 Tissue paper is a thin, translucent paper that is often used, folded or crumpled, for wrapping and cushioning delicate items for storage or travel. Tissue paper is also used in the process for making etchings and other fine art prints, as well as for dressmaking patterns. It is particularly

suited to projects that involve a lot of folding and creasing, especially pleating, as it takes on folds sharply and can be layered effectively.

5 Origami paper is available in three main types. The first, koi, is an easy-to-find, inexpensive, basic paper that is thin and easy to fold. The second type, Japanese foil paper, consists of a very fine sheet of paper covered with a thin layer of foil; it is good for holding folds. The third type, washi, is a thick handmade paper (see page 12), similar in texture to rice paper. Although very grainy, it is also very soft and holds origami folds well. It is rare to find these papers with a thickness greater than 1 mm but, although fine, they are quite strong and hard wearing.

6 Foamboard is a lightweight mount board made from polystyrene sandwiched between sheets of hot pressed paper. It is generally used for exhibition production, presentations and model making. Again, the thickness can vary, depending on the usage. Super fine, the thickness most often used for model making, is 2 mm; boards used for display purposes usually have a thickness of 10 mm. The most common thickness, available at most art stockists, and the one used in this book, is approximately 5–7 mm.

7 Brown packaging paper is also known as 'kraft' paper and is usually recycled. It's often used to make grocery bags and envelopes, as well as general packing. It is available in a range of weights and finishes, from the fine, which is used for crafting purposes, to the heavy, which has a slightly laminated, shiny finish and is much more durable and suitable for postage and packing. It has a utilitarian look to it, and is widely available from post offices, stationers and art suppliers.

8 Corrugated cardboard is a combination of paperboards – usually two fine, flat sheets and one inner fluted corrugated medium. The density can vary. The crafting variety tends to have a thickness of approximately 5 mm. That used for packaging is generally thicker and the corrugated inner section has larger flutes. The paper that it is sandwiched in is also heavier and the composite can have a thickness of 15 mm. It is mainly used for packaging on a large scale and is sturdy enough to build furniture.

PAPER RECYCLING

Recycling paper is a cost-effective and environmentally sound process, since, as it is not usually re-bleached, it produces fewer air-polluting elements in its manufacture and uses less water than normal paper. The use of waste paper to produce new paper also lessens disposal problems in terms of landfill. Paper cannot, however, be recycled indefinitely – perhaps five or six times – because each time it is processed the fibres within get shorter and thus weaker. At some point in the recycling process, virgin wood pulp has to be introduced to strengthen it again.

Newspaper, and in fact any recycled paper, is the ideal material for papier mâché, as the broken down fibres are exactly what is required to create a more malleable modelling substance. I also love using newspaper in more unusual, decorative ways – for decoupage, for example (see page 40) – or as gift-wrapping. Simply wrap a package with newsprint and add a decadent ribbon of velvet or satin. Newspaper is also ideal for inexpensive party decorations, such as the tree garland illustrated here.

OPPOSITE This garland is made by folding a length of newspaper, accordion-style, and cutting out a tree motif through the folded layers (see page 122 for template).

Paper techniques

PAPIER MACHE

Papier mâché is a simple way to make a versatile modelling material out of paper, which can be as light and delicate as a feather or have the consistency of clay.

To make papier mâché into a clay-like substance involves soaking newspaper in warm water, then blending it to make a pulp and squeezing out the excess water. Glue is then added to the mixture to give it some adherence.

The method I favour is the simplest, and even though the technique is one a young child could master, the results can be very sophisticated. It's a case of tearing strips of paper, soaking them in water and then laying them over a mould, and each other, until you have achieved the thickness you want, using either white glue or a diluted wallpaper paste as the adherent. I have used this method for a number of the projects in the book, including the tray, vessels and vase (see pages 32, 36 and 70), yet the effect for each is different, as the finished result is dependent on the type of paper used and the thickness of the layers.

Using an existing shape that you like as a mould is a great way to recreate and modify a design. When making the tray and vase mentioned above, I used existing ones covered in cling film as moulds, then layered over with paper. The cling film not only protects the mould, but also allows for easy removal of the dried papier mâché.

If you want to create a shape from scratch, be creative in your thought process and work out how a base or foundation can be built upon. I used a balloon as the base for the vessels, but you could also use fine chicken wire to create more elaborate shapes, and attach tape, card or rolled up newspaper to add more intricate embellishments.

Papier mâché can be strengthened using a method known as 'Japanning'. This involves applying several layers of varnish (either water-based PVA white glue or an oil-based wood varnish), which are left to dry after each application before applying the next. After several coats, the surface needs to be rubbed down lightly with a fine-grade sandpaper and wiped clean. Several more coats of varnish are then applied until the finish is rock hard.

PIERCING AND EMBOSSING

Piercing is an easy technique that can be used not only to add decorative detail, but also to allow light to peek through the paper, making it ideal for paper lampshades or screens.

The process for piercing flat and upright projects is similar. If piercing a flat sheet of paper, lay the paper on a soft background (a pile of newspaper, a thick piece of fabric or a blanket is ideal), then mark your pattern on the paper and, using a pin, make a hole, enlarging it if desired. When piercing an upright object, place something like Blutac behind the paper so when the pin goes through it is caught and stopped at the back, thus avoiding any injured fingers.

Embossing is usually done using a tool that is similar to a ballpoint pen, but obviously without

the ink content. Place the paper you wish to emboss, right-side down, on a soft surface, so that there is a little give underneath. Then, using some pressure, trace out your pattern. The drawing will transfer into a raised pattern on the reverse of the paper.

Another way of embossing is to imprint the paper with a pattern, by pressing the pattern into the paper. This can only be done on matt paper – paper that hasn't been coated or laminated – as a porous surface is needed. Spray a fine layer of water over the paper, just enough to make it damp and soft, but not so much that it gets wet. Take your motif, whether it is a coin, a card template or a wire twisted to make some kind of pattern, and lay it on top of the damp

paper, then sandwich the paper in between layers of scrap paper, soft fabric or a blanket. Finally, pile some heavy books on top and leave to dry, preferably overnight. When everything is removed, you should find that the pattern has been embossed on the paper.

Alternatively, use one of the many embossing kits available from craft suppliers. Use the rubber stamp to apply glue to paper in your desired pattern, then sprinkle the embossing powder over the glue. Blow away the powder from the unglued areas, and then subject the pattern to a heat source. This will cause the powder to melt and fuse over the glued area. When removed from the heat the melted glue and powder will harden into a raised pattern.

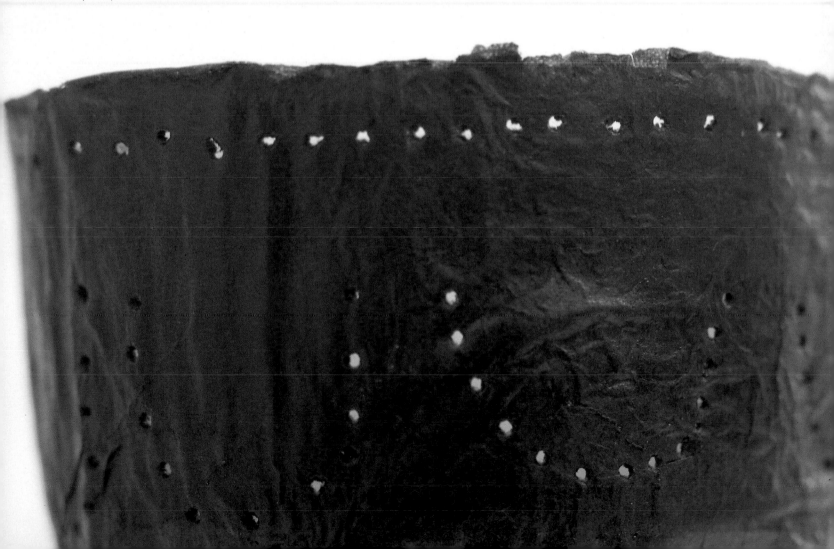

FOLDING AND CREASING

*When folding a sheet of paper or card, you need to first
work out which way the grain lies, as folding along the
grain will always give a smoother, sharper fold. If you fold
against the grain, the paper or card won't give as easily
and may buckle, giving an uneven crease.*

To find the direction of the grain, simply bend the sheet
of paper or card one way, without creasing it, then turn it
ninety degrees and bend it once more, again without
creasing it. At one of the two angles the paper will have
more tension and will spring back in protest – as you have
tried to fold the paper against the grain. The angle where
there is the least resistance is therefore the correct place to
fold it.

When folding and creasing paper or card, it is always
best to use a metal-edged ruler to fold the paper over to
an exact line, and then to use an implement of some kind
to press over the fold
to get a sharp, neat crease. You could use
a specific bone folder, which is one of many optional
crafting tools you can get. However, I find the handle of a
pair of scissors works just as well.

Paper folding can give a completely new dimension to a
flat sheet of paper. Known as origami in Japan, where it has
been practised for centuries, it is an art form in itself. An
understanding of the basic folding techniques (some of
which are illustrated on pages 118–21) allows for the
creation of numerous wonderful objects, including flowers,
birds and reptiles.

Once you have mastered the more complex techniques,
it is possible to create intricate projects involving hundreds
of folds – anything from a man with an umbrella to dragons,
skulls and insects.

PLAITING AND WEAVING

One of my favourite projects in this book is the plaited bowl (page 44). The method used to make it is simple, yet when the braids are sewn together, they take on a life of their own and form naturally into soft, organic shapes.

You can plait most types of paper, as long as they are flexible and fairly soft. The softer the paper, the easier it will be to plait, making tissue and newspaper ideal materials for this technique. It would be quite difficult, however, to plait stiff Indian khadi paper, as it isn't particularly malleable and tends to crease rather than fall into soft folds.

When plaiting, use the same technique you would use if you were plaiting someone's hair. Start with three strips of paper, clip them together at one end and then take the right-hand piece over the middle one, into the centre, then the left-hand one likewise, and repeat. You may find you need someone to hold the end when you begin, but, as you get down the length, you can clasp it between your knees until you reach the other end. Braided lengths of paper can then be sewn together to make a variety of items. Placemats, similar to those woven from rattan, are what come to mind immediately. The method is exactly the same as used for the bowl, but instead of manipulating the circle up, make sure it lies flat. Individual lengths of braid would also look great stretched across a frame to make a screen.

Weaving can be used to add texture, if you are using same colour papers, or to create a more graphic look, if you are using strong contrasting colours, as in the chessboard project (page 48). The basic method used for the chessboard is very straightforward, and involves cutting several strips of paper, all measuring the same width. Begin by placing one strip running down one edge of the cardboard being used as your base, then another strip joining it at the corner, but running down the adjacent edge. It is then just a case of weaving each strip you lay down under and over the strip next to it. Once you have mastered the basics, you can experiment using not only different widths of paper, but also different textures and patterns, such as tartans, plaids and checks.

CUTTING AND THE RIGHT EQUIPMENT

Although this may sound too basic for discussion, cutting the paper correctly and with the right equipment will make creating these projects very much easier.

Ideally, you should have several pairs of scissors, including wallpapering scissors, which have very long blades and are good for cutting large sheets of paper, and a regular, medium-sized pair of scissors with very sharp blades. A small pair of nail or embroidery scissors, which are good for cutting tiny and intricate details, are also very useful. Try to ensure that the scissors you use for your paper crafting are kept separate from other household scissors, because they need to be kept as clean and as sharp as possible. Always use separate scissors to cut tape because the sticky residue can adhere to the blades.

You will also need a craft knife or scalpel, with plenty of spare blades, together with a cutting mat. I use a scalpel for most of my cutting as, in most cases, you can achieve a more precise cut. It is particularly difficult to cut a straight line with a pair of scissors, as you have to move the scissors along without an aid. With a scalpel, you can cut in one smooth, continuous movement, using a metal-edged ruler, as well as the ruled lines on the cutting mat, as a guide.

It goes without saying that these blades are extremely sharp and you should always try to cut diagonally away from yourself, to avoid any slips. Change the blades often, as a used, blunt blade will pull and drag at the paper, making your cut uneven and messy.

When cutting out a symmetrical motif, a handy tip is to fold the paper in half first and to draw half your motif onto the folded edge of the paper. Cut around the drawn line and then unfold the paper to reveal a perfectly symmetrical cut-out – you can see how this is done in the paper-cutting project on page 74.

DECOUPAGE

Decoupage, which comes from the French word 'decouper', meaning 'to cut out', is the craft of decorating an object – often furniture – with paper cut-outs. Traditionally, each layer is glued onto the surface and is then sealed with several layers of varnish until the stuck-on pieces of paper attain the appearance of inlay work or painting. During the eighteenth and nineteenth centuries it was an extremely popular pastime, so much so that decoupage scraps were produced especially for this craft.

I'm not one for sticking to traditions, so my version of this decorative craft is much more graphic. Instead of the cupids, hearts and filigree patterns favoured in the past, I think that making your own, less fussy motifs, using solid silhouettes cut out of coloured papers is the way forward. For the project on page 40, I used newsprint as the base and plain coloured motifs of linear stems and soft undulating flower heads.

Nor do I tend to varnish as much as is traditional. Obviously, if the item is going to come in for a lot of wear and tear, go ahead and varnish away – just make sure that you allow each coat to dry thoroughly before you apply the next. Once you have achieved a good build-up of varnish, you can lightly sand the edges of the decoupage image to lessen and flatten off the edges so that it looks as if it's painted on. Make sure to wipe it clean, though, before you resume varnishing.

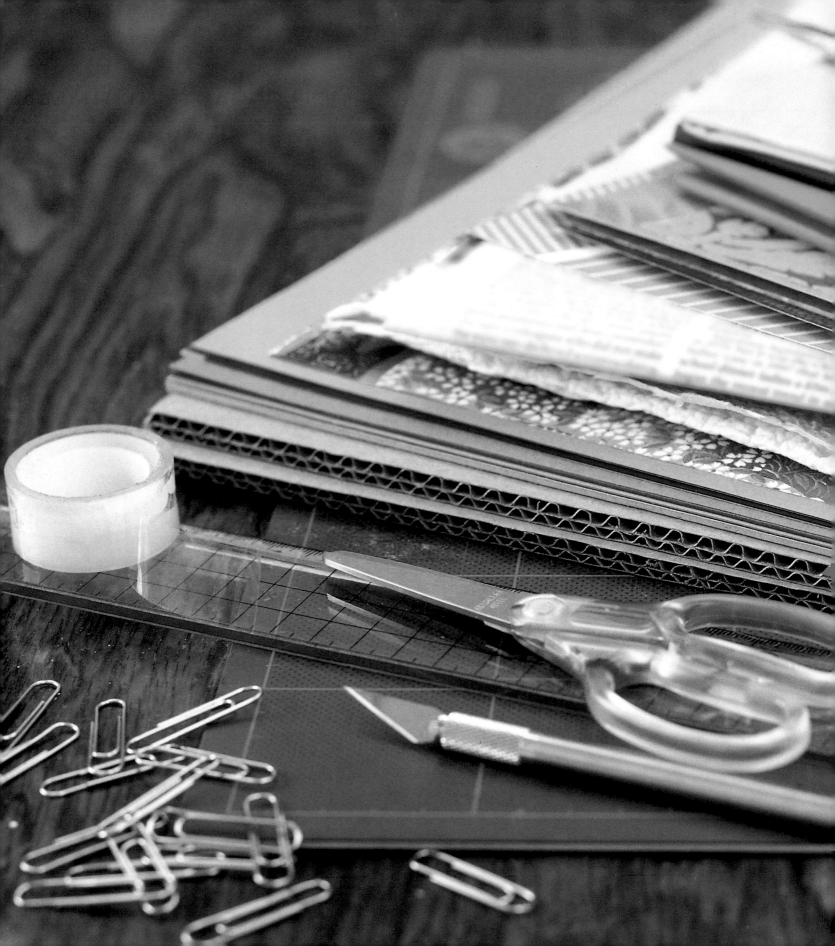

The projects

Layering and weaving

Paper tray

This tray is made from layers of humble brown packaging paper, and uses an existing wooden tray as the mould.

Because I have used torn strips of brown 'kraft' paper (the alternative name for packaging paper), which in itself is a recycled product, the final effect is very natural looking. The strips should be torn to lengths that are slightly longer than the radius of the tray, so that when you are layering them, overlapping the strips in a circular manner, they automatically make up the rough edges, giving the tray a tactile finish. If the strips are too long, they can be torn to the right size whilst the paper is still wet, but avoid having them too short, as you will then have to resort to patching up the holes.

As the papier dries around the mould, the paper contracts and puckers to give a creased surface, adding to the organic look.

YOU WILL NEED
- *Tray to use as a mould*
- *Cling film*
- *10 x A2 sheets brown packaging (kraft) paper*
- *Wallpaper paste*
- *Paintbrush*
- *1 x A3 sheet medium density card (2 mm thickness)*
- *Scissors*
- *PVA or white glue*

Step 1

Cover the tray in cling film; this will make it easier to remove the dried papier mâché from the mould. Tear the brown paper into strips approximately 60 cm long and 5 cm wide. Mix up some very diluted wallpaper paste using approximately 1 part granules to 10 parts water.

Step 2

Paste the first strip and lay over the cling-film-covered tray, from the centre to the edge. Begin to layer strips, fanning them across the centre as you go until the tray is completely covered. Continue going around until you have at least six layers of paper strips. Leave to dry completely.

3

Step 3

Using a plate with a diameter of 24 cm as a template, draw and then cut out a circle of card. Stick this onto the back of the tray using PVA or white glue. This will give the tray its solid base.

Step 4

Carry on layering pasted paper strips over the cardboard circle, as before. In order to make the tray sturdy, you will need to apply at least ten layers (the more you apply, the thicker and sturdier it will become). Allow to dry completely, then pull gently away from the mould. The ends of the paper should be left rough, for a natural-looking finish. If you think they look too messy, just tear them down to even them out. Finally, seal the tray (so it can be wiped clean) by painting over a layer of white glue. This will go on white, but will dry to a clear, varnished finish. Alternatively, you could use spray acrylic varnish to seal.

4

Papier-mâché vessel

The beauty of papier mâché is that it can be manipulated in so many ways. Traditional papier mâché is sturdy and, in its heyday as a building material, was heavily lacquered to give it the appearance and strength of wood or plaster.

Here, the papier mâché isn't pretending to be anything other than what it is – paper. I wanted these vessels to be as light as a feather and almost translucent, as if they were about to float away. The paper I used is a translucent, fibrous paper, which is almost as fine as tissue. I simply layered roughly torn strips over inflated balloons to create these organic, bulbous shapes. Obviously, the shape you end up with depends on the size of the balloon, and the transparency on the number of layers of papier mâché you apply. You can make sets of vessels by blowing up balloons that vary in size, and also achieve different finishes by using alternative papers.

YOU WILL NEED
• 1 x A1 sheet textured
  fibre paper
• Balloon
• Wallpaper paste or
  PVA/white glue
• Bowl of warm water
• Paintbrush

Step 1

Tear the paper into rough strips approximately 15–20 cm in length and 5 cm in width. There is no need to be too exact about this. Blow up your balloon, to the size you want your vessel to be. If you are making a set of vessels, inflate several balloons in varying sizes.

Step 2

Mix up some very diluted wallpaper paste using approximately 1 part granules to 10 parts water. Alternatively, you can use a diluted solution of PVA and water. Quickly soak each strip of paper in warm water to make it softer and more pliable, then layer onto the balloon, applying paste both onto the balloon and over the strip using a brush. Repeat with all the strips, layering, overlapping and smearing them with paste as you go, making sure to leave an opening at the top. Leave to dry.

Step 3

Make sure the papier mâché is bone dry before popping the balloon and revealing a delicate, decorative vessel. If the balloon pops as the vessel is drying, as can sometimes happen, don't panic. Just remove the balloon, place another inside the vessel and inflate it – the vessel will expand back out with the blown-up balloon.

Decoupage chair

This simple white dining chair has been customised so it doesn't look like the thousands of identical chairs found in dining rooms across the country.

You can guarantee that you won't find another one like it.

To decorate something decoupage style using a foreign language newspaper means that you don't have to concern yourself with what the text running across it actually says and can instead concentrate on it looking good. Plus there's something aesthetically pleasing about an exotic newspaper, though I can't quite put my finger on exactly why. Perhaps it's because you imagine you're looking at an opinion on international politics from a foreign point of view, when in reality you're looking at an advertisement for hair transplants!

I've used a Chinese language newspaper to completely cover the back and seat of the chair, lining the pieces to the edges, and overlapping the paper where gaps appear. Any newspaper or magazine with interesting letters would work. Recently I went into a Turkish comic book store and noticed they had covered the benches with pages from random comics – and enjoyed myself trying to figure out the conversations relating to the illustrations.

YOU WILL NEED
- *Dining chair with a solid chair base and back*
- *1 x foreign language newspaper*
- *Blutack*
- *PVA/white glue*
- *Small brush*
- *1 x A2 sheet pink textured paper*
- *Scissors*
- *Scapel or craft knife*
- *Cutting mat*

Step 1

Cut out sections of the newspaper and arrange them around the chair back and base, using Blutack to stick them in place until you are satisfied with the arrangement. Once you are happy with the position of the newspaper, brush a thin layer of white glue over the chair and begin to paste the newspaper sections into place.

Step 2

Cover the entire chair in the newspaper, overlapping the pieces where gaps appear, and lining them up to the edges of the chair. Push out any air bubbles that form, popping the ones that are more difficult to remove with a pin. Allow to dry thoroughly. In the meantime, begin to prepare the flower motifs.

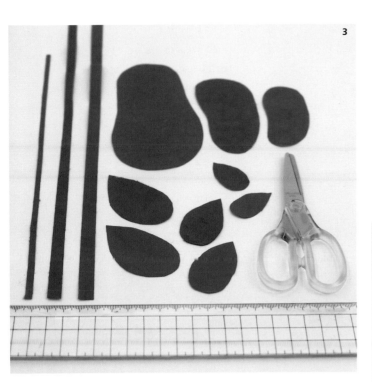

Step 3

Using the templates on page 122, cut three strips of the pink paper with widths of 5 mm, 1 cm and 1.5 cm. Each strip should be a little bit longer than the last. Also cut three pairs of leaves and three oval flower heads. Again, each pair should be a bit larger than the previous one. Depending on the size and shape of your chair, you may need to adapt the templates.

Step 4

Place the stems, leaves and flower heads on the chair base and back – again using Blutack to position them until you are happy with the arrangement – then carefully glue them into position, pushing out any air bubbles that form (using a pin if necessary). Allow the glue to dry, then seal by pasting a thin layer of PVA over the entire chair This will go on white, but dry to a clear, varnished finish.

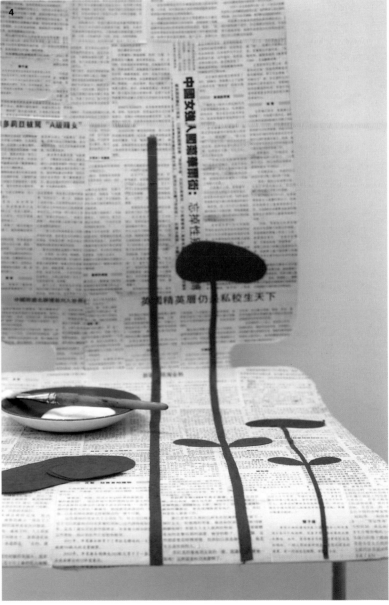

Plaited bowl

This bowl was inspired by one that I found in Tanzania, which was made from plaited, recycled electrical wires.

For my version, I've used plaited strips of paper, which I've sewn together in concentric circles. While I was sewing the strands together they naturally formed into a bowl shape, in a fairly organic manner; all I had to do was to gently ease them into the required shape.

The bowl I've made here is quite small – about the size of a cereal bowl – and it requires approximately 8–10 strands of plaited paper. You could easily make something larger, like a fruit bowl, though it would obviously need more strands of plaited paper (about 20–30), as well as more time and patience.

I've made the bowl using both newspaper and tissue paper, to show how different it can look. The newspaper gives it a monochrome feel, whereas the tissue paper makes it much softer in texture. If you wanted, you could also use a glossy magazine, which would give it a harder edge.

Step 1

Unfold the tissue paper and cut out strips approximately 1.5 cm wide across the length of the sheet, to get the longest possible strips. Take each strip and fold it in thirds lengthways, so that the raw edges of the paper are folded in and the paper has a bit more strength.

Step 2

Take three folded strips, pinch all three together at one end and secure with a paperclip. Now begin to braid: take the right strip over the middle strip, then the left one over the middle one, and repeat, keeping the braid as tight as possible without pulling and ripping the paper. Repeat with the remaining strips until you have enough lengths of braided paper for the size of the bowl you want to make – about eight braids for a cereal bowl, 20–30 braids for a fruit bowl.

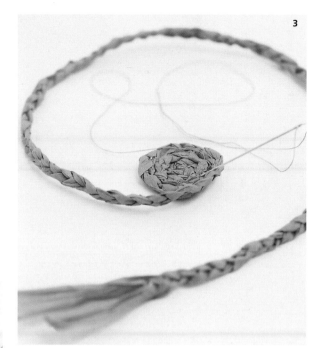

Step 3

Now start making the actual bowl by curling the first braid in on itself to create a flat circle. Using a needle and thread, sew the outer circle around the edge of the inner circle.

Step 4

When you get to the end of the first braid, take another, sew the free ends to each other, and continue to sew the braid around the edge of the inner circle.

Step 5

If you intend to make a larger bowl, keep the first few braided circles as flat as possible. When the base has a diameter of roughly 4 cm, begin to manipulate each length so it curves slightly upwards. It's a case of gently pulling up the sides as you sew. In this way you can make the bowl more oval or shallow or deep, depending on the shape you prefer.

Chess set

This chess set is a project of two halves — the pieces, which consist of cardboard covered in layers of tissue, and the board, which is made of woven strips of paper.

The pieces are cut from one sheet of dense card; with the exception of the bishop, they are then folded together and taped closed. The bishop pieces are slightly different in that, once cut, the two identical pieces of card are slotted together, to form a cross shape. Every piece is then covered in layers of tissue paper, which not only covers up the tape, but also smoothes the edges and adds colour. I used pale duck egg blue and dark golden brown tissue papers.

The chessboard is made by weaving two different kinds of paper over a corrugated cardboard base. Although the method is fairly straightforward, it may take some time (and patience) to ease the strips of paper into an exactly symmetrical woven square. Ensure you don't pull too hard, or the paper will tear.

The woven board can be adapted to make placemats; the 32 cm square used here is the ideal size for a 24 cm dinner plate, but it can be made larger if you want a serving mat or smaller if you require a coaster.

Step 1

Using the templates on page 123, trace the chess figures (two kings; two queens; four rooks, knights and bishops; and 16 pawns) onto the medium density card, then cut out.

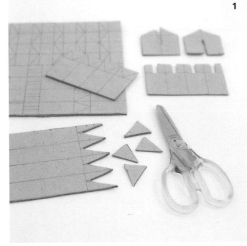

YOU WILL NEED

- 1 x A3 sheet medium density card (2 mm thickness)
- Pencil
- Ruler
- Scissors
- Craft knife
- Cutting mat
- Masking tape
- 5 x A2 sheets tissue paper of each colour
- Corrugated cardboard measuring 32 cm square
- 1 x A2 sheets paper in each colour
- Paintbrush
- PVA or white glue
- Double-sided tape

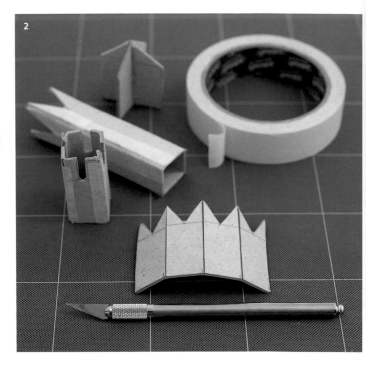

Step 2

Once each piece has been cut out, score lightly along the dotted (fold) lines using a craft knife. Fold together to form 3-D shapes and then, using masking tape, tape securely together, ensuring that the pieces stand upright and straight. Slot together the two identical bishop pieces and ensure that they, too, stand upright.

Step 3

Divide the chess pieces into two sets, put one set aside, and begin working on one colour first. Cut the tissue paper into thin strips and, using white glue, simply paste all over each piece. You want the colour to become opaque, so you will need to add several layers. Paste a layer of white glue over the final layer to seal. Repeat with the second set using the other colour tissue paper. Set aside while working on the board.

Step 4

Cut eight strips of brown and eight strips of blue paper, each measuring 40 x 4 cm. Starting with a brown strip, place it along one edge of the corrugated cardboard square. Allow it to overlap it at the top by 4 cm, and tape the excess to the underside of the board. Now take a blue strip and place it at right angles to the adjacent edge of the board. Thread the end underneath the brown strip so it, too, overlaps by 4 cm and tape this excess to the back of the board. Take another blue strip and place it alongside the first blue strip, so that it extends over the brown strip, and again tape it to the underside of the board.

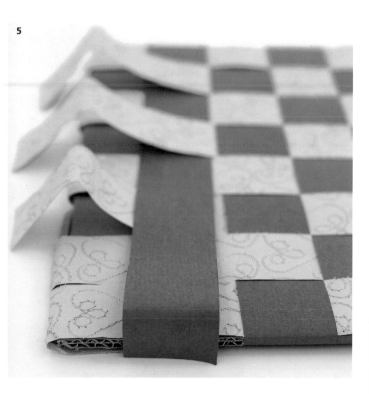

Step 5

Repeat this process, alternating between the blue and brown strips. When you have finished, secure all the loose ends to the underside of the board with masking tape.

Step 6

Turn the board over. Cut a piece of blue paper 30 cm square and apply double-sided tape all around the edges. Remove the backing from the tape and stick the paper down so that it hides all the overlapped strips on the underside and gives a neat finish.

Cutting and piercing

Placemat

Eating at my local branch of Wagamama, where the turnover of customers is fast and the ordering speedy, inspired this very quick and easy project.

The Wagamama placemats are made of paper sheets and your order is scribbled onto them so the waiter always knows who's ordered what. I took this idea and expanded on it. I replaced the untreated paper with a laminated khadi paper, so the placemat could be wiped clean, and added a pocket – which is sewn into place using paper twine – for cutlery or chopsticks. The large running stitches remind me of the first sewing projects I made when I was at school, and add a certain naïve, funky charm.

This is another project that could be embellished quite easily. The mats would make great table settings for a party – a baby shower, a girls' lunch or a child's birthday, for example – and instead of having place cards the person's name could be written on the mat with chalk or using stickers. The mats could also be decorated by either stapling or sewing on paper flowers.

Step 1

Using a ruler as a guide, tear the waxed paper into two rectangles measuring 50 x 30 cm. What you want are neat, but rough, torn edges. Set one rectangle aside.

1

2

Step 2

Tear the khadi paper into two rectangles measuring 22 x 12 cm. Set one aside. Fold over one of the short ends by 3 cm, then fold this flap over on itself to make a kind of hem. Place in the right-hand corner of the waxed paper rectangle, approximately 2 cm in from each of the edges.

Step 3

With the twine, and using a medium-sized running stitch, sew the khadi paper patch onto the waxed paper, about 0.5 cm in from each edge. Leave the top end open to make a pocket. Repeat for the other placemat.

3

Wall hanging

This project was inspired by patchwork quilts and is a great way of displaying a collection of postcards that might otherwise languish in a drawer. Here I used a collage of my favourite cards with a toning colour palette.

In addition to postcards, I used lots of individual card stock pieces, as well as the occasional piece of metallic card, which I cut to the same generic postcard size (approximately 15 x 10 cm). I then punched holes along the sides where they were to be attached, reinforced these holes to stop them from ripping, and then linked them on all sides with copper rings to create a 'curtain'. If you can't find copper rings, do what I did and twist copper wire around a pencil or thin cylinder and cut off individual rings.

If you prefer, the wall hanging can be put to a more practical use, by suspending it over a door as a partition. In this case don't attach the cards side to side, only from top to bottom, so they can be separated when you walk through. You could even use transparent card or paper to make it into a window screen.

Step 1

You will need 36 pieces of card for this project: seven postcards, two metallic cards and 27 stock cards. Put aside the postcards and then, using either scissors or a craft knife, cut the desired number of 15 x 10 cm rectangles from the sheets of stock card and metallic card.

1

Step 2

Now punch holes in the cards, strengthening them with adhesive reinforcement rings. Most of them will have four holes, one in the middle of each edge. The cards running down the right-hand side will have three holes – on the top, lower and left-hand edges. Those running down the left-hand side will have three – on the top, lower and right-hand edges. The cards making up the bottom row will have three holes each, but they will be on both sides and the top edge. The bottom corner pieces need only two holes, one each on the inner edges.

Step 3

Line up the cards in the correct order, according to the punched holes and what looks pleasing to the eye. Then begin to join the cards to each other by slipping the copper rings through the holes.

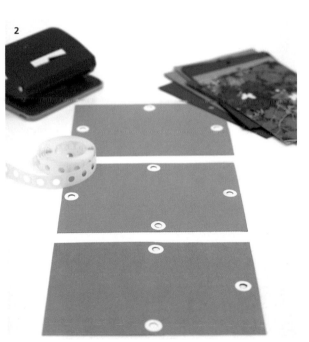

Step 4

Build up the collage of cards so that you have six cards going across and six down, looping them together with the rings as you go. Loop the rings along the top of the top row of cards and thread them through the Perspex rod. Hook onto a wall or suspend from the ceiling.

Lampshade

Paper has been used in lighting for centuries, especially in the Far East. We are all familiar with the white paper balls – the Akari – variations of which can be picked up cheaply at most hardware stores, and also the brightly coloured, festive Chinese lanterns that expand, accordion-style.

Paper is the ideal material to work with when making lampshades – it not only diffuses light perfectly, but also comes in various weights, from almost completely transparent to virtually opaque. Its one, fairly obvious, drawback is that it is flammable, though the degree of flammability varies according to type. You should therefore consider carefully your choice of paper when embarking on this project. The most suitable is probably washi, a Japanese paper made from mulberry bark, which is readily available and comes in a variety of finishes and weights. Another good choice is Japanese rakusui 'veil' paper, which is what I've used here, as it diffuses artificial light to a soft glow. You should avoid using rag papers, as these tend to have a high cotton content (and are therefore more flammable). It's also a wise precaution to invest in some flame retardant spray – available from upholstery and theatrical supplies shops – and to use a low-wattage light bulb.

YOU WILL NEED
- *15 x 12 cm rectangular lampshade frame*
- *1 x A0 sheet white Japanese rakusui 'veil' paper*
- *Ruler*
- *Pencil*
- *Scissors*
- *Paper glue*

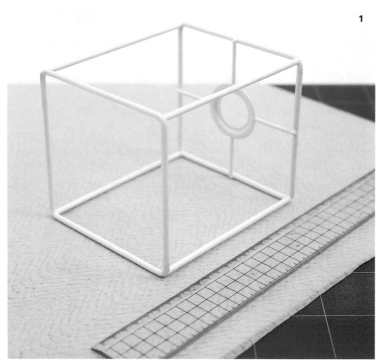

1

Step 1

Work out how long you would like the 'drop' on the shade to be before you start – it can be made either longer or shorter depending on where you intend to hang it. The drop here is 45 cm. Once you have decided, fold the rakusui paper in half and measure 45 cm (or whatever length you prefer) from the fold, so you actually have a 90 cm length of paper, folded in half.

2

Step 2

Using a pencil, mark off 60 strips, approximately 1 cm in width. Carefully cut out, from the fold down, through the double thickness of the paper. Keep the strips folded.

Step 3

Apply paper glue to the frame, then, keeping it folded, lay a paper strip over the frame, slightly overlapping the folded edge at the top. Pinch the overlap and the strip together, to completely cover this section of the frame. Pull the strip down over the lower part of the frame and glue the inner strip to this part of the frame (this will prevent the paper from flapping onto the light fitting once it is hung), leaving the outer strip hanging free.

4

Step 4

Continue to attach the folded strips of paper until none of the frame is visible and you have a layered, fringed shade. Hang the shade up and trim to whatever length you like.

Calendar

This multi-year calendar is based on a simple rotating device and was inspired by an old-fashioned telephone.

Even the colours of the materials that I have used – the copper-coloured metallic card and the textured black paper – are reminiscent of the old style of telephones. The materials also add a real tactile edge to it, so that when you put your fingers into the holes to turn the calendar to the correct date it feels good.

Making the calendar is fairly straightforward. Once you have ensured that the circles of card and paper are the right sizes, and have established the centre point of each, it is relatively simple to line them up correctly with each other. However, it takes time, patience and a steady hand to apply the numerals. I recommend first working out where each one goes before starting to add them. I used an old-fashioned graphic design Letraset®, but, if you can't find Letraset®, stickers will do the job just as well. Alternatively, you could draw the numerals in by hand. The finishing touch is the insertion of a brass-coloured butterfly paper fastener through the centre.

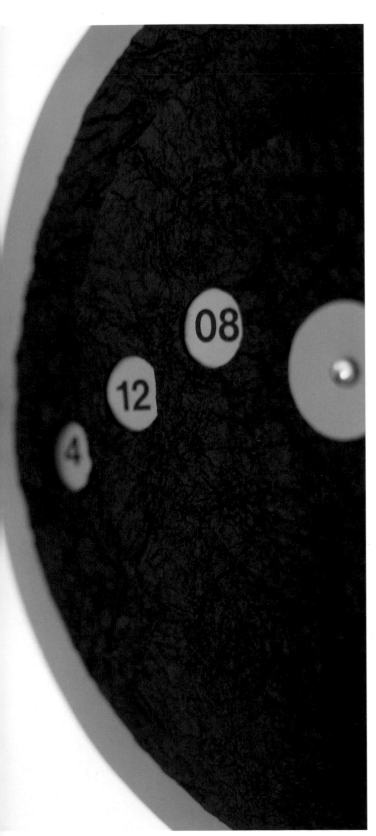

YOU WILL NEED
- *2 x A2 sheets copper-coloured metallic card*
- *1 x A2 sheet textured black paper*
- *Compass and pencil*
- *22-cm single hole punch*
- *Scissors and craft knife*
- *Letraset® transferrable numerals and rubbing implement*
- *Brass butterfly paper fastener*

Step 1

Using a compass, draw three circles on the metallic card, with radii of 14, 10.5 and 7 cm, and cut out using sharp scissors. Do the same on the textured paper. Mark the centre points of each circle and score a tiny cross through each with a craft knife.

1

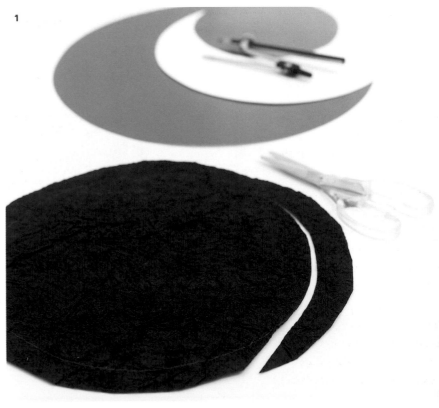

Step 2

Take all three textured paper circles and punch a hole in each one, 1 cm in from the edge.

2

3

Step 3

Using adhesive numbers, put the relevant day, month, and year numerals around the edges of the three metallic card circles. The largest circle will be used for the days, the middle one for the months, and the smallest for the year. Use the black paper circles to help you position them correctly.

Step 4

Place the largest paper circle on top of the largest card circle. Place the middle-sized card on top, followed by the middle-sized piece of paper, the smallest card circle, and finally the smallest paper circle. To finish, cut out another circle from the metallic card, with a radius of 16 cm, and lay it underneath the other circles. Take a brass butterfly paper fastener, push it through the centre and open it out at the back. Rotate the circles to show the correct date.

4

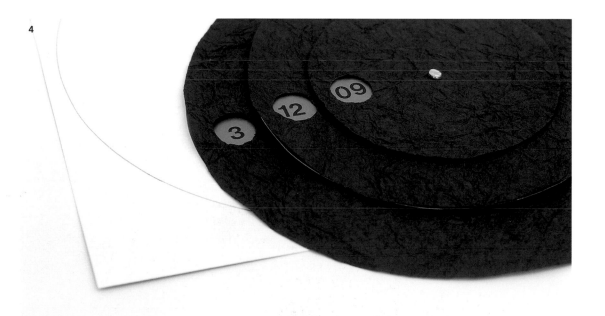

Beaker

I have a real soft spot for the old-fashioned, decorative metal water beakers that my parents had when I was growing up. But these days, even when trawling through the markets in Pakistan, they are quite difficult to find.

The modern versions just don't have the delicate, decorative edges that I remember, so I decided to make my own version out of papier mâché, using tissue paper. Of course, being made of paper, the beakers aren't exactly practical for drinking from, but, if you put a glass inside them, they make cute little vases.

I used a ceramic pint beaker as my mould, though you could easily use something larger or smaller. Because the tissue paper is so fine, and likely to stretch and tear when it is damp with paste, you need to patch over the inevitable tears as they happen using small pieces of tissue. The number of layers you apply will determine how fine or dense your beaker is. The finishing touch is the tiny pin-prick pattern along the upper rim, which allows the light to filter through the delicate edges.

YOU WILL NEED
• 10 x A2 sheets black
  tissue paper
• Pint beaker
• Cling film
• Wallpaper paste
• Paintbrush
• Blutack
• Thick pin

Step 1

Step 2

Roughly tear a circle of tissue paper, large enough to cover the beaker. Mix up some very diluted wallpaper paste, using approximately 1 part granules to 10 parts water. Brush the beaker with paste, place it in the centre of the circle of tissue paper and bring up the sides of the tissue so it covers the mould.

Step 3

Tear the tissue paper into fine strips. Brush the wallpaper paste over the beaker and begin layering with the strips, using your fingers to mould them to the shape of the beaker. Don't worry if the tissue rips, just continue layering, doing one layer vertically and the next horizontally. You can patch up any tears as you go along. Continue until you have applied at least 20 layers. To speed things up, you could do the first few layers in tissue, and then the next several in newspaper, finishing off with the tissue. This will have the added benefit of making the finished article stronger.

Step 4

Leave the beaker in a warm place to dry completely (this could take up to two days). Gently prise the beaker away from the mould; you may need to insert a fine knife between the cling film and the mould to help ease its release.

4

5

Step 5

With a thick pin, pierce a pattern along the rim of the beaker, and another below, following the contours of the mould, going from the outside inwards, using a small piece of Blutack at the back as a buffer. If you prefer, mark out the pattern with a pencil first.

Paper-cutting picture

Paper-cutting is a decorative technique found in many places across the world. Each country has its own particular, distinctive style, but the basic method is similar everywhere.

Although the oldest surviving paper-cutting picture is from the sixth century, and was found in China, the most well-known paper-cuttings come from Mexico, where is is known as papel picado, and Poland, where it is known as wycinanki. In Mexico, it is used to stunning effect during the celebrations for the Day of the Dead, when paper skulls, skeletons and other macabre effigies are used to decorate homes. In Poland, paper-cutting is equally popular. Before glass became widely available, sheepskin was hung in farmhouse windows, in which small opening were cut using sheep shears to let in light and air. Over time, these cuts became decorative as well as practical, and although paper later replaced sheepskin, large shears are still used in traditional Polish paper-cutting.

The motifs most commonly found in Poland are flowers and birds, and they are the inspiration behind my own, very simple paper-cut. I am not an expert, but, as you can see, even the most inexperienced paper-cutter can come up with wonderful silhouettes, which look very effective when worked with a contrasting colour in the background.

The materials I have given are enough to make all the motifs. I was able to find a multiaperture frame, but you could equally easily use several frames to display your finished piece.

Step 1

Using the template of the bird on page 124, trace the motif onto tracing paper using a soft pencil. (This is used so that when the trace is turned over and drawn over the pencil lines will transfer cleanly and visibly onto the poster paper.) Cut a rectangle of turquoise paper measuring 16 x 9 cm and fold it sharply in half, right sides together (using scissor handles or something similar to achieve a clean fold). Place the tracing paper, drawn-side down, over the folded paper, making sure that the bird's beak abuts the edge of the fold (so that when it is cut out you end up with a perfectly symmetrical motif). Now trace over the motif, again using the soft pencil. This will transfer the design onto the back of the paper.

Transfer the designs for the other motifs in a similar way, varying the colours of the motifs and backgrounds, though note that none of these additional designs need to be traced onto folded paper as complete templates have been given.

Step 2

Place the turquoise paper with the bird motif onto the cutting mat and carefully cut it out using a craft knife or small, sharp scissors if you prefer. Make sure that the tips of the beaks at the fold remain joined together. Also cut out and remove the 'wing' sections, the eyes, and the tail feathers. Unfold the cut-out image to reveal an exact symmetrical image.

Cut out the other motifs in a similar way.

Step 3

Lay the various motifs on the appropriate backgrounds, which need to be cut to the size of your frame(s). Once you are happy with the position of everything, stick the motifs onto the backgrounds with either paper glue or spray adhesive. Allow to dry completely before inserting in your frame.

3

Wall feature

This striking wall feature is made from heavy cream khadi paper, which has been stretched and stapled onto a large, square frame.

The idea for this piece came about when I was doing the paper-cutting project and noticed the way in which the paper flicked up while I was cutting it, producing an interesting three-dimensional effect. I took this spark of an idea and ran with it, experimenting with different ways of encouraging the paper cut-outs to remain erect. I eventually came up with the idea of this tightly petalled flower, which consists of rings of semi-circular cuts. The sophisicated white-on-white gives the project a discreet look, but if you wish it could be made more noticeable by hooking some low-wattage fairy lights behind it to illuminate it. If you opt to do that, make sure the paper you use isn't flammable, either by spraying it with a suitable fire retardant or by choosing a paper that has already been treated.

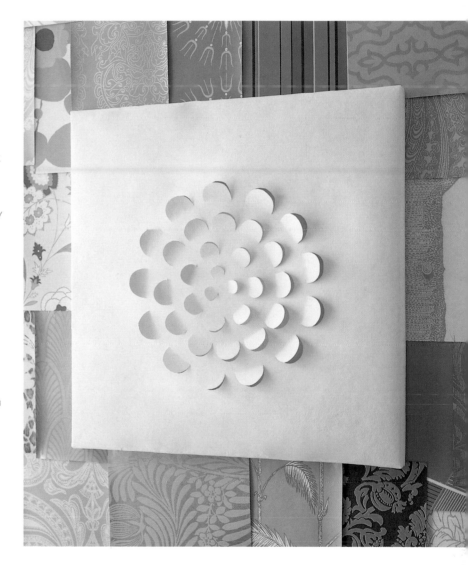

YOU WILL NEED

- *60 cm square wooden frame/artist's stretching frame*
- *Scissors*
- *1 x A1 sheet of cream khadi paper, medium to heavy thickness*
- *Pencil*
- *Compass and/or circular templates decreasing in size: plates, bowls, cups, bottle tops, etc.*
- *Eraser*
- *Cutting mat*
- *Craft knife*
- *Staple gun and staples*

Step 1

Begin by putting the frame together – an artist's stretching frame is ideal as the pieces just slot into place. Put it on top of the paper and draw around the inner frame; you will need to keep within this area when marking out your design. Trim the paper around the exterior frame, leaving an allowance of approximately 7 cm so that the paper can be wrapped comfortably over the frame later. Put the frame aside and begin to work on the flower pattern. Using a compass, draw a circle with a diameter of 40 cm in the centre of the marked square. Then, using a small cup as a template, draw evenly spaced semi-circular 'petals' around the edge of this circle.

Step 2

Using plates and bowls as templates (or a compass if you prefer), draw seven more circles, decreasing in diameter width by approximately 5 cm, evenly spaced inside the first, large circle. Then using cups and bottle tops, mark further small, semi-circular 'petals' evenly spaced around the edges of two more concentric circles.

2

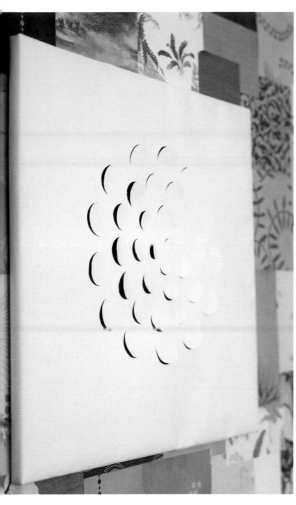

Step 3

Place the cutting mat underneath the paper and carefully cut out the semi circles using a craft knife.

Step 4

When all these have been neatly cut, take an eraser and rub away all the excess pencil markings, apart from the initial square.

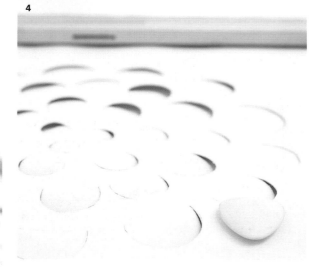

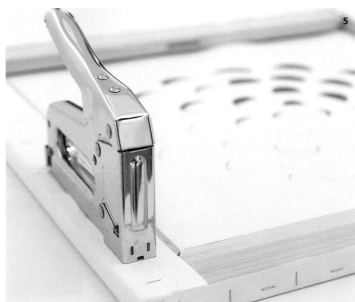

Step 5

Place the frame over the paper, matching up its inner frame to the pencil square. Fold over the edges and staple into place along the back or edges of the frame, making sure that the paper isn't pulled too tightly and stays smooth. Turn the frame over so the right side is facing you and gently manipulate the cut-out semi-circles so that they curl up, creating three-dimensional petals.

Folding and pleating

Paper flowers

Colourful and enormous fun, these beautiful, large, dahlia-inspired
tissue paper flowers are simple and bold.

Not dissimilar to the woolly pompoms you may have made at school, they
consist of sheets of fine-pleated tissue that are tied together with florist's
wire and then carefully pulled and tweaked out to form three-dimensional
spheres. They work particularly well as table decorations, and are just perfect
for a wedding or other festive occasion, either suspended in a cluster from
above or placed in a row down the centre of a table. They look very
effective when you have a mixture of bright primary colours, as here, though
they take on a completely different feel when they are made in softer pastel
colours or all in white. They also make brilliant decorations for a child's
room, either as large pompoms or suspended as a mobile over a baby's cot.

Step 1

Take several sheets of tissue paper and, beginning from one of the shorter edges, make a fold of approximately 2.5 cm, then fold this pleat back on itself. Continue to 'accordion pleat' across the whole sheet, placing a sharp crease at each fold. If you want to vary the size of your flower, cut the sheets down before you start to fold them over.

Step 2

Mark the centre of the folded strip, pinch it together to make it narrower, then wrap a length of florist's wire around the centre, twisting it tightly. Using a sharp pair of scissors, trim each end into petal shapes. I have made pointed petals, but you could also make them rounded or scalloped.

Step 3

Now, starting on one side, gently begin to separate out the petals. Pull each layer of tissue paper away from the centre, one at a time, taking care not to tear the paper, and puffing up the petals as you go.

Step 4

Repeat with the other side, pulling out and manipulating the tissue until you have a spherical flower. To finish off, attach a length of monofilament thread to the centre (where the florist's wire is holding the flower together), from which to suspend it.

Wall tidy

The idea for this project came to me when I was looking for a way to use some of the gorgeous wallpaper swatches I have acquired.

One of them, from Cole and Son, had a particularly appealing geometric motif, which was perfect to decorate this simple, graphic wall tidy.

The tidy is made from an uncut sheet of black foamboard, on which I've laid strips of copper-coloured, metallic card, behind which you can tuck postcards, invitations, etc. These strips are held in place at the back with Sellotape, and at the crossover points on the front with drawing pins. I've also added two pockets with vents, again made from wallpaper swatches, which can hold light items.

This type of board is ideal to use as a noticeboard since the foam has some give in it, which allows drawing pins to be inserted and removed with ease. However, unlike a cork board, the holes aren't self healing, so if you do use pins, be aware that this will shorten the life of your wall tidy.

Storage boxes

Inspired by the panettone boxes that are so abundant at Christmas time, these have a nice shape to them and can be made up in any size.

Here, I have made a set of storage boxes in various colours, which I've tied with a variety of ribbons. They would work equally well, however, as small gift boxes or wedding favour boxes, in which you could put sugared almonds or petits fours. Another alternative is to make them smaller still, from metallic card, and hang them on a Christmas tree. Instead of using ribbons as the ties, you could make loops out of decorative twine or tinsel, and instead of almonds place secret treats or chocolates inside. You could go further and add numerals to the boxes, so they could be used as an Advent calendar.

The instructions given are for a box approximately 16 cm square, but all you need to do is either enlarge or reduce the template to arrive at the size you require.

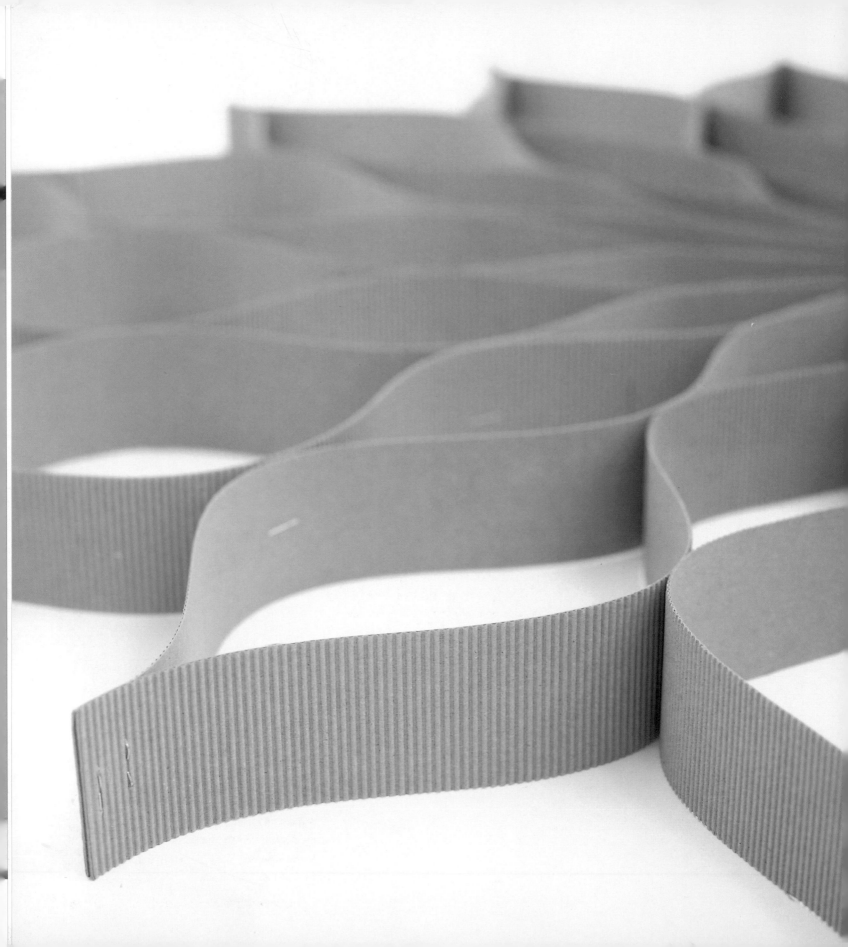

1

YOU WILL NEED
- 1 x A1 sheet fine craft corrugated card
- 1 x A3 sheet fine, stiff white card
- 1 x A4 fine, stiff recycled card
- Stapler and staples
- Ruler
- Pencil
- Scissors
- Glue
- 6 cm square quartz clock mechanism and hands

Step 1

Cut 15 strips of the corrugated card, across the grain, each measuring 100 x 5 cm. Fold each strip in half and staple together 2.5 cm away from the fold. Then staple again 20 cm away from the fold, and 2.5 cm away from the open end. Each strip should have two openings.

2

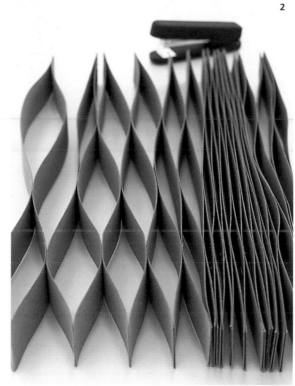

Step 2

Line up all the strips side by side, with the cut ends together at one end. Using a stapler, attach each strip to its neighbour at the midpoint of each opening. Each strip should have two staples attaching it to the next. When all the strips have been stapled to each other, they should resemble an accordion when pulled out.

3

Step 3

Measure the dimensions of the clock mechanism, then cut a shallow rectangular section half its length and depth out of the cut ends of all the strips. These cut ends will eventually form the centre of the clock, where the mechanism slots in. Now gently pull out the openings at the top, and bring the ends together to form a circular flower. Staple the two free sides together, as you did earlier.

4

Step 4

Using a 24 cm dinner plate as a template, cut a circle out of the white card, then glue it, centrally, to the back of the clock. Cut another 12 cm circle out of the recycled card and pierce a hole in the centre. Slot the clock mechanism into the cut-out section at the front of the clock and place the card over it. Slot on the clock hands.

Foamboard table

Foamboard consists of a sheet of foam sandwiched between two sheets of fine paper and is the perfect material for making this table.

Generally used for mounting artwork and displays, it is fairly sturdy, cuts cleanly and works well as a construction material – ideal qualities for this clever little side table. The density of the board requires some cutting, known as mitring, to allow it to fold correctly. This is a fairly involved technique that may need a bit of practice to get right. The trick is to score the folded points gently, so the cut doesn't go through to the back of the paper, and then to carefully cut away the foamboard from either side of the score, so that when you fold the board together it forms a neat, condensed fold.

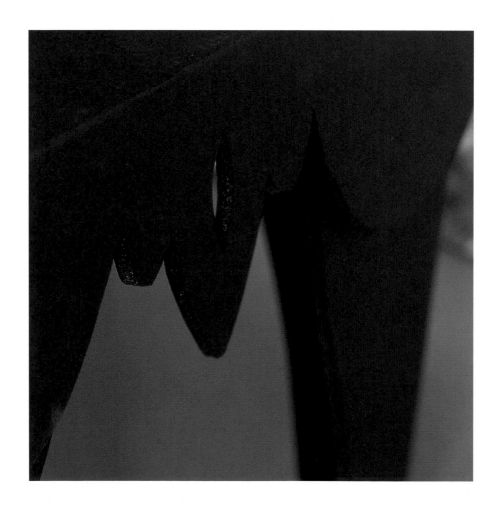

YOU WILL NEED
- *3 x A0 sheets strong foamboard (2 for the legs and 1 for the table top)*
- *Pencil and paper*
- *Craft knife*
- *Cutting mat*
- *Ruler*
- *Strong black gaffer tape*

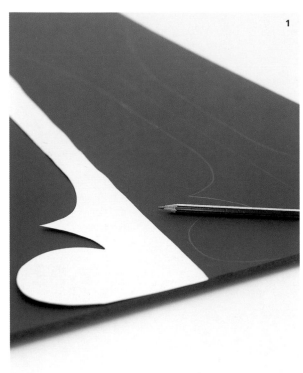

Step 1

Using the template for the leg on page 126, draw around it once, then flip it over and draw around it again, to create a mirror image. The line running down the centre marks where the fold will be. Carefully cut out using a craft knife. As the board is quite dense, you may need to score through it several times in order to do so. Repeat for the other three legs.

Step 2

Using a craft knife, carefully score along the centre line of each table leg in one smooth movement, making sure that you don't cut through to the paper on the other side. Holding the blade at a 45 degree angle, cut a triangular strip from either side of the line and remove the excess foam. This mitre will make folding the leg easier.

Step 3

Fold the legs so the two sides form a right angle and the mitred edges meet. Tape into position using gaffer tape along the entire length of the legs.

Step 4

Draw a 30 cm square in the middle of the third sheet of foamboard, then add a 10 cm allowance to each edge (so you have another 50 cm square surrounding it). Line the template for the scalloped edge (page 126) up against the inner square and draw around it. Flip it over and repeat around the table top. Carefully cut out the scalloped edge.

5

4

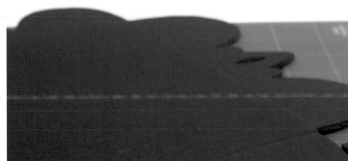

Step 5

Now score the underside of the inner square in the same way you did the legs, taking care not to cut all the way through the foam. Cut away triangular strips on either side of the scored line to form mitred inner edges. Fold the scalloped edges so they are at right angles to the table top and the mitred edges meet. Tape into position using gaffer tape.

6   ## Step 6

Place a leg in each corner of the table top and tape securely into position using gaffer tape.

Photo frame

This picture frame has five apertures, which can be folded up, rather like an accordion. If you wish, it can be made larger or smaller to incorporate as many or as few photographs or postcards as you like.

You can also vary the size of the apertures to accommodate an unusually large or small print or photograph, or one that is an odd shape.

The base of the frame is made from five separate pieces of cardboard (the type used for packaging and boxes) that are attached to each other with gummed brown paper tape. The pieces need to be separated like this so that they can fold with ease; if it were made of just one piece of card it wouldn't fold, nor would it stay upright. I then covered the cardboard with a lizard print paper that I found in the gift-wrap department of a large stationery store – at first glance the frame looks as if it's made from leather. In the same store I found mock croc, snake and ostrich skin wrapping papers, but the frame would look equally good in any kind of printed paper – flock would work particularly well.

YOU WILL NEED
- *1 x A1 sheet corrugated cardboard (packaging type)*
- *Pencil and ruler*
- *Craft knife*
- *Cutting mat*
- *Gummed brown paper tape*
- *2 x A2 sheets printed paper*
- *Paper glue*
- *Scissors*
- *Sellotape®*
- *Double-sided tape*

Step 1

Cut five rectangles of cardboard for the backs of the frames, measuring 13.5 x 18 cm. Cut a further five rectangles of cardboard measuring 13 x 17.5 cm for the fronts.

Step 2

Take the pieces for the front and rule lines 2.5cm in from the edge on all four sides. Cut out the inner rectangles to make the apertures for the frames.

Step 3

Lay the pieces for the backs vertically side-by-side, with a gap of approximately 5 mm between each of them. Using the gummed tape, attach the pieces to each other at the sides, taking the tape all the way around, from the front to the back. Once you have done this, bend the pieces back and forth to make sure that they fold comfortably. Also check that they can stand upright.

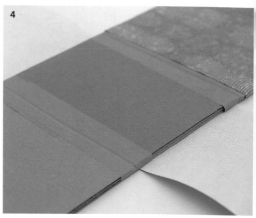

Step 4

Cut three lengths of printed paper measuring 13 x 40 cm. Wrap these around the three centre pieces of the frame, overlapping the ends, so that they cover the entire front and back, and glue into position. A small amount of gummed tape should still be visible at the sides where the frame folds.

Step 5

Cut two pieces of printed paper measuring 14 x 40 cm and cover the two end pieces of the frame, tucking the ends in for a neat finish. Put this five-part, 'hinged' piece aside.

Step 6

Cut another rectangle of paper, measuring 16 x 20.5 cm. Place one of the aperture pieces on the back of the paper and then wrap the paper over the sides, mitring the corners. For a neat finish, first cover each inner corner with a tiny tab of paper so that, eventually, when you complete the wrapping of the piece, none of the cardboard will be visible. Repeat with the other four aperture pieces.

Step 7

Cut an 'X' through the paper covering the aperture, running diagonally from inner corner to inner corner. Take one of the triangular sections of paper, fold over the point, then fold it back over the side of the aperture, covering the inner edge and securing it in position with Sellotape®. Repeat with the other three triangular sections, so that the aperture of the frame is fully and neatly covered. Repeat with the other four aperture pieces.

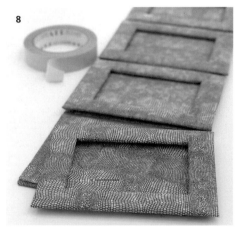

Step 8

Place strips of double-sided tape on the side and bottom edges of each aperture piece, leaving the top edges free. Stick onto the hinged back section, positioning the free edges along the top to allow your pictures to be slid in and out easily.

Photo album

I felt I couldn't do a book about paper without at least dipping my toe into the art of bookmaking.

This is one of the simpler ways of making a book, but it is still fairly complicated as there are so many components to it. Given the time it takes, and the fact that it's possible to buy reasonably inexpensive photo albums, it's important that anything you make should reflect your particular tastes and use beautiful materials. I started off by deciding to use this gorgeous Japanese printed paper, which was simply too beautiful to wrap a gift in and give away. I also chose high-quality 'mi-teintes' paper (which is usually used as a drawing paper for pastels and chalk) for the pages, so that the difference between them and the translucent interleaves was noticeable. All the pages are sewn into the spine of the book, which, like the rest of the cover, is made from corrugated cardboard. The various pieces of the cover are then joined together using gummed brown paper tape.

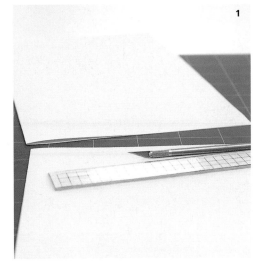

Step 1

First cut the pages to size. Fold a sheet of the mi-teintes paper in half lengthways, then mark along the folded edge and top edge of the paper at 25 cm intervals. Rule a line from top to bottom and carefully cut three pieces of paper.

YOU WILL NEED
• 3 x A1 sheets lily-white mi-teintes paper
• Ruler and pencil
• Craft knife
• Cutting mat
• 1 x A1 sheet corrugated packaging cardboard
• Needle
• Buttonhole thread
• Brown paper gummed tape
• 1 x A1 sheet decorative paper
• Scissors
• Double-sided tape
• 3 x A1 sheets translucent paper

Step 2

Slot these pages inside each other. Repeat with the remaining two sheets of paper so that you end up with three sets of six pages.

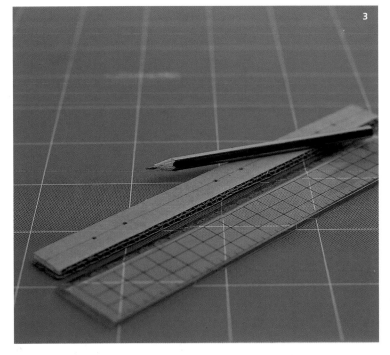

Step 3

Cut a strip of cardboard measuring 25 x 2 cm. Rule a line down the centre and mark points 3 cm in from each end, then 5 cm in from each end. Find the centre and mark points 1 cm on either side of this. Using a sharp pencil, pierce holes through the cardboard at each of the six points (you will probably need to turn the strip over and pierce through again to make the six holes).

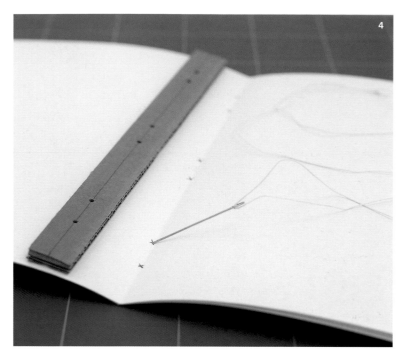

Step 4

Mark the same points down the centre fold of the three sets of pages, making sure that, when laid side by side, the points on the three sets align. Pierce holes through all the points with a needle.

Step 5

Using a needle and thread, sew the first set of pages together through the paired pierced holes, and then through the same holes in the spine, so they are attached. Repeat with the other two sets of pages, so that all of them are sewn through the same set of holes on the spine. Neaten the top and bottom ends of the spine by covering them with a small piece of gummed tape.

Step 6

Cut two pieces of cardboard measuring 26 cm square. Also cut two strips measuring 2 x 26 cm, and a third strip measuring 2.5 x 26 cm. Lay the pieces out flat, with one square piece on the left, a 2 cm strip next, the 2.5 cm strip in the middle and then the second 2 cm strip and the other square on the right side. Separate each piece slightly from the next, leaving a gap of 0.5 cm between each one.

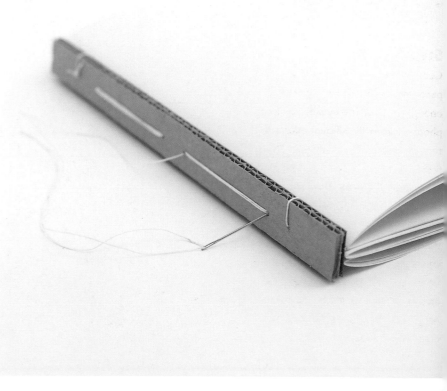

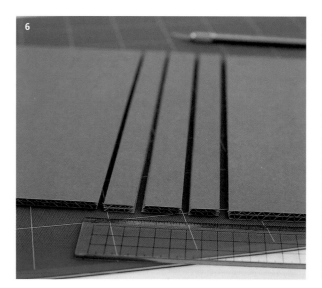

Step 7

Join the pieces together using gummed tape, taking the tape all the way around, from the front to the back. Once you have done this, bend the pieces back and forth to make sure they fold comfortably. The middle section will become the spine of the book; the two strips on either side allow the covers to be opened and closed easily.

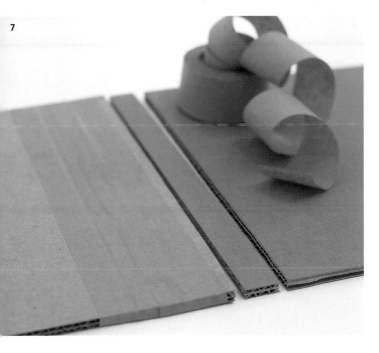

Step 8

Cut three strips of decorative paper, two measuring 2 x 30 cm and one measuring 2.5 x 30 cm, and glue onto the segmented spine, folding the excess ends over and sticking them to the inside of the cover.

Step 9

Cut two rectangles of decorative paper measuring 40 x 31 cm. This is enough to cover the outside of the photo album with sufficient excess to turn the paper over neatly. Glue the first piece to the left-hand side of the cover, lining it up very close to the spine, but leaving a gap of 5 mm. Fold over the three other sides, securing them to the inside of the cover with tape. Repeat on the right-hand side. Glue squares of paper to cover the cardboard left exposed on the inside. Attach the pages to the spine using double-sided tape.

Step 10

Cut 17 pieces of translucent paper for the interleaf pages, each measuring 24 cm square. Take each of the pieces, lay double-sided tape along one of the edges and attach to the mi-teintes paper at the inner left-hand edge of each facing page, though not to either the first or the last page.

Crane mobile

The flying crane, a symbol of longevity, is probably the most well known of the traditional Japanese origami figures.

Indeed, ancient Japanese legend says that anyone who folds a thousand origami cranes will be granted a long life by the crane. The word origami is derived from the Japanese words 'oru', meaning to fold, and 'kami', meaning paper. Although its origins are unclear, papermaking is thought to have originated in China and to have spread to Japan by the sixth century. Models were not initially diagrammed, but were taught from one generation to the next. Paperfolding was gradually incorporated into many aspects of everyday life in Japan, where it continues to be used not only for decorations, but also for envelopes and packages. There are a handful of basic folds that you need to master, which, although they may seem difficult at first, will, after a few attempts, become second nature.

YOU WILL NEED
• *5 sheets origami paper,*
  18 cm square
• *Needle and thread*
• *45 cm wooden*
  dowelling, 1 cm thick
• *Jigsaw*
• *Matt black paint*

1

Step 1

Begin by folding a sheet of paper in half diagonally, then in half diagonally again, to make a triangle.

2

Step 2

Open out the second fold and squash it down, lining up the centre crease with the fold beneath it. This will form a square. Turn over the paper and repeat the procedure so that you have what is called a square fold.

Step 3

Fold the right- and left-hand flaps of the top layer so they meet in the centre. Turn over the paper and repeat on the other side so you have a kite shape.

3

4

Step 4

Take the top small triangle and fold it down, making a crease, then unfold. This is done to make a folded marker for the next stage. Repeat the procedure on the other side.

5

Step 5

Open the whole thing back out to the square fold. Using the crease mark made in the previous step, lift the bottom corner of the top layer up and back on itself; the prepared crease mark will help you to manipulate the paper. Push the flap right to the top and then press the right- and left-hand sides to the centre to create a thin diamond shape. Turn it over and repeat the procedure on the other side.

6

Step 6

Fold in the outer edges of the top layer so that they meet in the centre, turn over and repeat on the other side.

Step 7

You will now have an even narrower, thin kite shape, with a lower section that is separated at the centre. Fold these separated pieces up to the centre, so that the 'arms' stick out on either side, then let them fall back down. This is to create a crease mark for the next step.

7

Step 8

Open out the top section, pull one of the 'arms' up and fold along the crease that you have just made. Close the flap around it. Repeat this with the other 'arm'.

8

9

Step 9

Take one of the arms, which should now be poking out of the sides of the flaps, and make a slanted fold halfway down it. Unfold it and then fold it back in on itself to create the crane's head.

Step 10

Now take each flap and pull them out and down, to make the wings. As you pull, you will see the finished crane emerge. Gently expand the crane's back and curl the wings and tail.

10

11

Step 11

Take a needle and thread, knot the thread at one end, then pierce the crane from the underside, bringing the needle up and out of its back.

12

Step 12

Mark the midpoint of the dowelling, then mark points 8 cm and then 16 cm either side of this. Using a small jigsaw, cut five notches into the dowelling at these points. Also cut notches 2 cm in from each end of the dowelling. Paint the dowelling with the black matt paint, then allow to dry. Tie two lengths of thread onto each end, bring them to the middle, tie them together and hook up so the dowelling hangs straight and balanced. Then take each crane and tie into place, staggering the lengths of the thread so that they look as if they are flying in sequence.

Templates

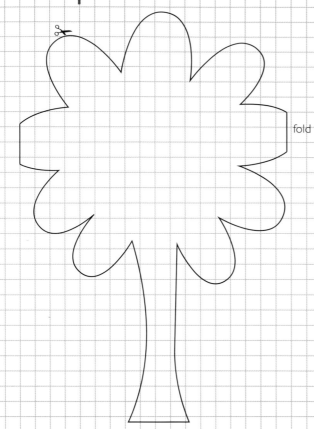

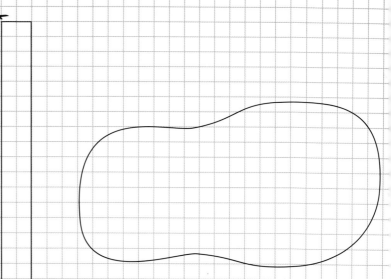

fold

Flower head: make one at 100%, one at 125%, and one at 150%.

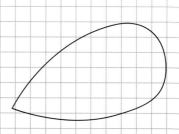

Leaves: make two at 100%, two at 125%, and two at 150%.

TREE GARLAND

Take a sheet of newspaper and cut it horizontally into three strips. Stack the strips and fold them accordion-style. Place the template on top, ensuring that the dotted lines align with the folds on either side, and draw around it. Cut through all the layers, taking care not to cut the folded edges. Open the paper to reveal three rows of trees and tape together to make one long garland.

Stem: Make one with a width of $\frac{1}{4}$ inch (6mm), one with a width of $\frac{1}{2}$ inch (1.3cm), and one with a width of $\frac{3}{4}$ inch (2cm). At line, add or subtract length according to the size of the chair.

CHESS PIECES

4 x Rook

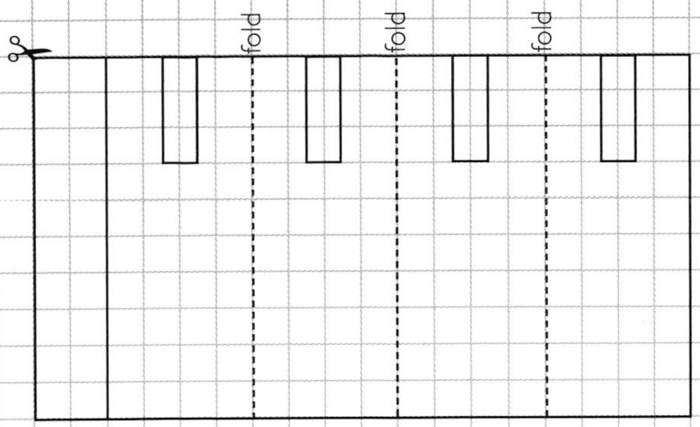

4 x Bishop

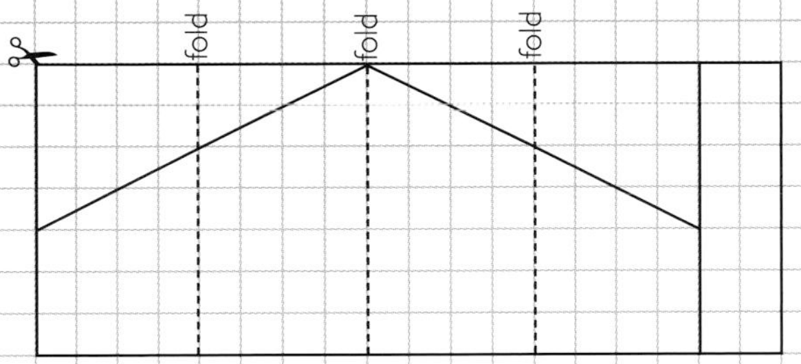

16 x Pawn

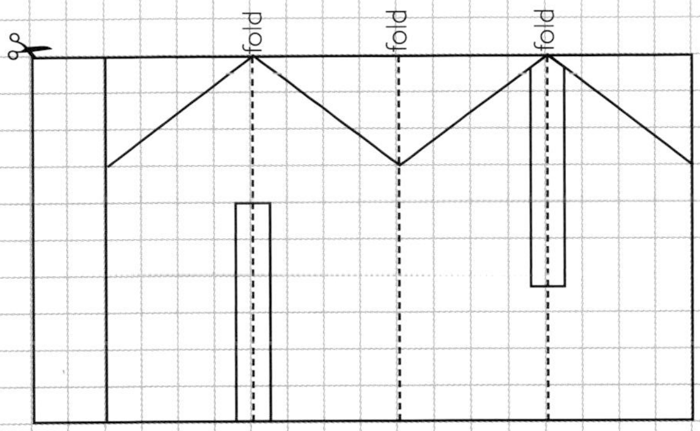

4 x Knight

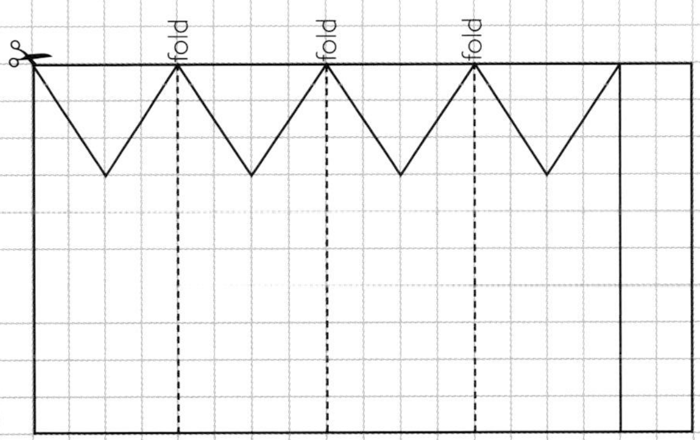

2 x King

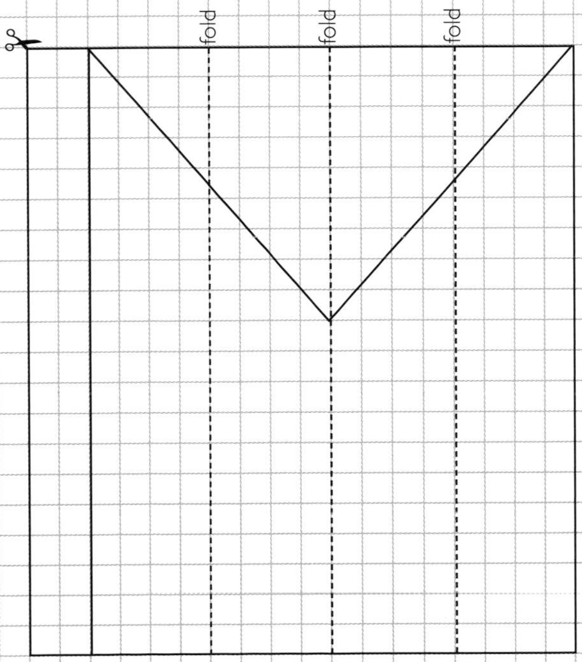

2 x Queen

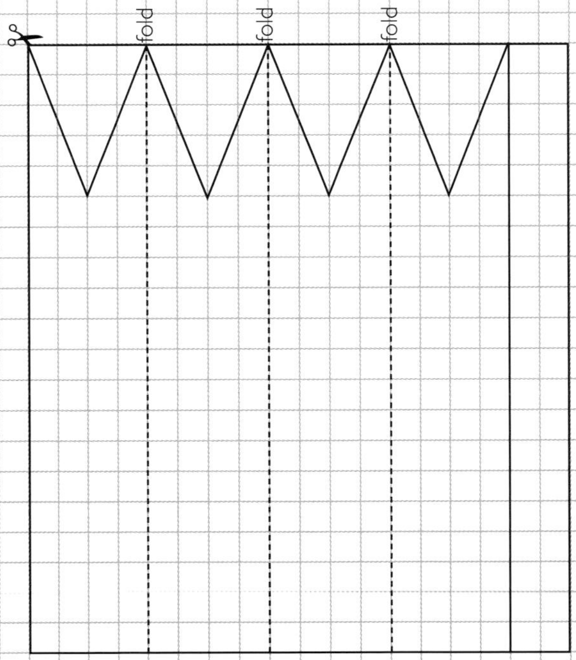

PAPER-CUTTING

tip of beak on fold

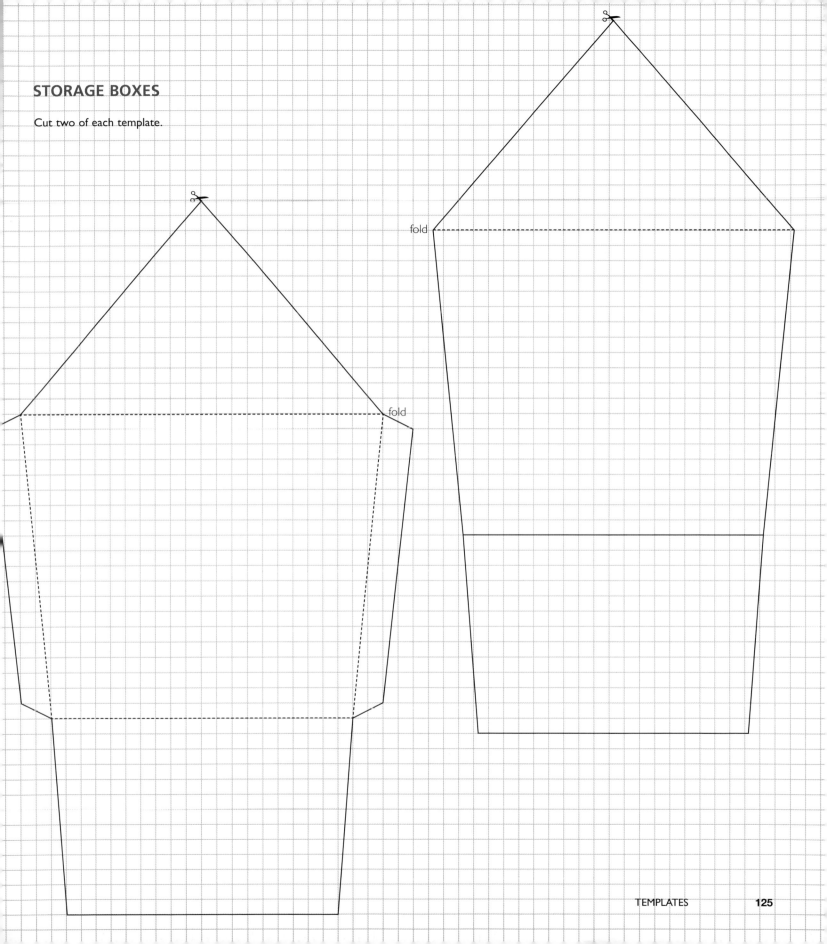

STORAGE BOXES

Cut two of each template.

fold

fold

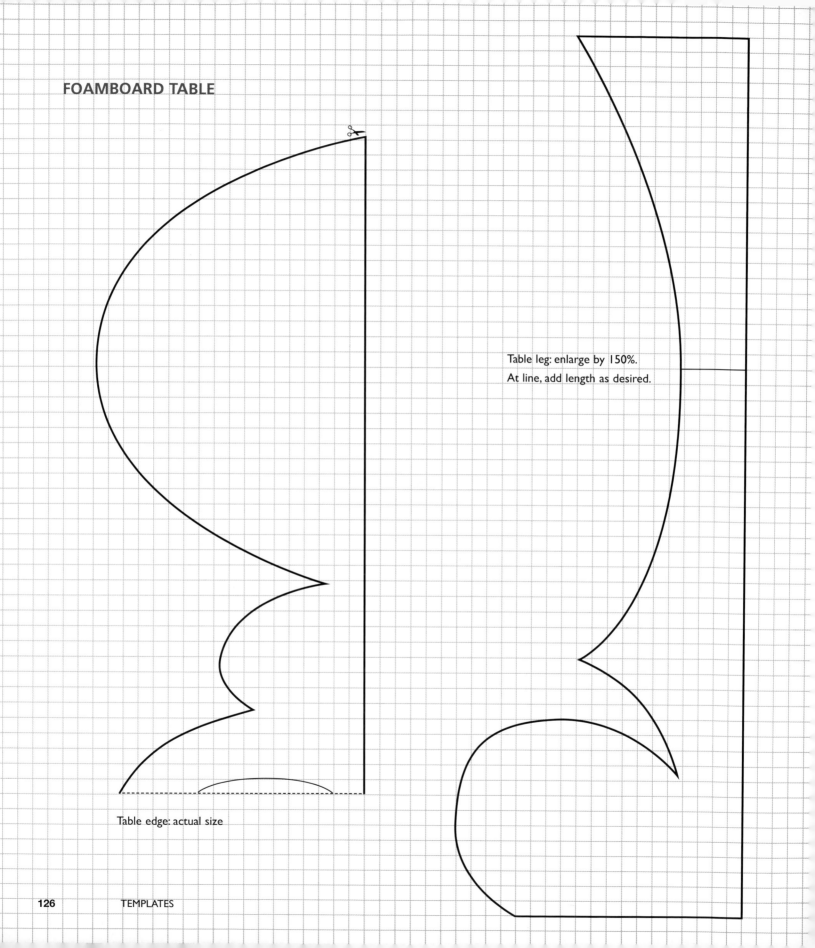

FOAMBOARD TABLE

Table leg: enlarge by 150%.
At line, add length as desired.

Table edge: actual size

Stockists

The paper and adhesives used in this book should be available at your local paper, craft or office supply store or online. If you cannot find them, please contact the following companies.

ATLANTIS EUROPEAN
7–9 PLUMBERS ROW
LONDON E1 1EQ
TEL 0207 377 8855
Every art supply you can imagine and a great range of papers

BUREAU
10 GREAT NEWPORT STREET
LONDON WC2H 7JA
TEL 0207 379 7898
Good selection of papers, cards, gift wrap and art materials

COLE AND SON
www.cole-and-son.com
Wallpapers, with a huge back catalogue of classic designs

THE CONRAN SHOP
MICHELIN HOUSE
81 FULHAM ROAD
LONDON SW3 6RD
TEL 020 7589 7401
www.conran.com

L. CORNELISSEN & SON
105 GREAT RUSSELL STREET
LONDON WC1B 3RY
TEL 0207 636 1045
www.cornelissen.com
Selection of papers and craft tools

COWLING AND WILCOX
26–28 BROADWICK ST
LONDON W1V 1FG
TEL 0207 734 9557
www.cowlingandwilcox.com
Specialize in watercolour and cartridge papers

FALKNER FINE PAPERS
76 SOUTHAMPTON ROW
LONDON WC1B 4AR
TEL 0207 831 1151
Traditional papers and book binding

FLAVOR PAPER
4213 CHARTRES STREET
NEW ORLEANS
LA 70117
TEL 001 1 504 944 0447
www.flavorpaper.com
Bespoke wallpapers

FRED ALDOUS
PO BOX 135
37 LEVER STREET
MANCHESTER M60 1UX
TEL 0161 236 2477
All kinds of crafting equipment and art materials

HOBBYCRAFT
www.hobbycraft.co.uk
TEL 0800 027 2387
Craft superstore

HOLLOWAY ART AND STATIONERS
222 HOLLOWAY ROAD
LONDON N7 8DA
TEL 0207 607 4738
Watercolour papers, art paper and materials

JESSIE CHORLEY
www.jessiechorley.com
Decoupage and scrap booking journals, secret boxes and jewellery

JOHN LEWIS
OXFORD STREET
LONDON W1A 1EX
TEL 0207 629 7711
www.johnlewis.com
Good stationery department

LONDON GRAPHIC CENTRE
16–18 SHELTON STREET
LONDON WC2H 9JL
0207 240 0095
www.londongraphics.co.uk
Graphic design and craft tools, paper art materials

THE PAPER SHED
www.papershed.com
Range of papers and cards

PAPERCHASE
213–15 TOTTENHAM COURT RD
LONDON W1T 9PS
TEL 0207 467 6200
www.paperchase.com
Huge selection of art materials, papers, stationery, gifts

TRACY KENDALL
www.tracykendall.com
Bespoke wallpapers

VITRA
30 CLERKENWELL ROAD
LONDON EC1M 5PG
TEL 020 76086200
www.vitra.com
The original George Nelson Sunflower Clock

WOOLWORTHS nationwide
www.woolworths.co.uk
TEL 0845 608 1101
Basic stationery items

Acknowledgements

First of all, I would like to thank my good friend Janine Hosegood for her gorgeous photographs and, for being such a calming influence and a pleasure to work with, as always. Also to Sarah Rock, who worked so hard to design such a beautiful book, through it's many incarnations!

A special mention to the press offices at Paperchase and Vitra. Paperchase, for providing many of the papers used throughout this book, and especially to David, who went out of his way to be helpful in preparing the huge loans I took out! And also to Tricia at Vitra, for being so helpful in providing permission for me to illustrate my version of the Sunflower Clock.

Happy birthday to Aneela, my oldest friend, who always goes out and buys my books!

Last but not least, to Basharat — who I didn't know when I first started working on this book, but is now my wonderful husband. Love you, Mr Din.